The Penang Adventure

A History of the Pearl of the Orient

The Penang Adventure

A History of the Pearl of the Orient

RAYMOND FLOWER

Cover photograph from Getty Images.
Cover design: Benson Tan

This book published by Marshall Cavendish Editions
An imprint of Marshall Cavendish International
1 New Industrial Road, Singapore 536196

Other Marshall Cavendish Offices
Marshall Cavendish Ltd. PO Box 65829, London EC1P 1NY, UK • Marshall Cavendish Corporation. 99 White Plains Road, Tarrytown NY 10591-9001, USA • Marshall Cavendish International (Thailand) Co Ltd. 253 Asoke, 12th Flr, Sukhumvit 21 Road, Klongtoey Nua, Wattana, Bangkok 10110, Thailand • Marshall Cavendish (Malaysia) Sdn Bhd, Times Subang, Lot 46, Subang Hi-Tech Industrial Park, Batu Tiga, 40000 Shah Alam, Selangor Darul Ehsan, Malaysia

National Library Board Singapore Cataloguing in Publication Data
Flower, Raymond, 1921-
The Penang adventure : a history of the pearl of the Orient / Raymond Flower. –
Singapore : Marshall Cavendish Editions, c2009.
p. cm.
Includes bibliographical references.
ISBN-13 : 978-981-261-886-3 (pbk.)

1. Pinang – History. 2. Ethnic groups – Malaysia – Pinang.
I. Title.

DS598.P5
959.51 — dc22 OCN458439734

Printed in Singapore by Utopia Press Pte Ltd

DEDICATION

When back in the mid-eighties, I mentioned to Sjovald Cunyngham-Brown that I was thinking of writing a book about Penang, he sportingly suggested that we should do it together. Sjovald had been the penultimate British governor of Penang, and had just finished a biography of Francis Light. It was a privilege to collaborate with him and I have pleasant memories of the convivial meetings at which, gin-and-tonics in hand, we thrashed out the details of our story. Sadly, however, Sjovald died suddenly in the spring of 1988, and it was only 20 years later, when Penang was awarded World Heritage status by UNESCO, that I thought of reviving the project. Needless to say, his detailed notes proved invaluable; so the least I can do is dedicate this book affectionately to the memory of my good friend and former co-author, Sjovald Cunyngham-Brown.

Raymond Flower
March, 2009

CONTENTS

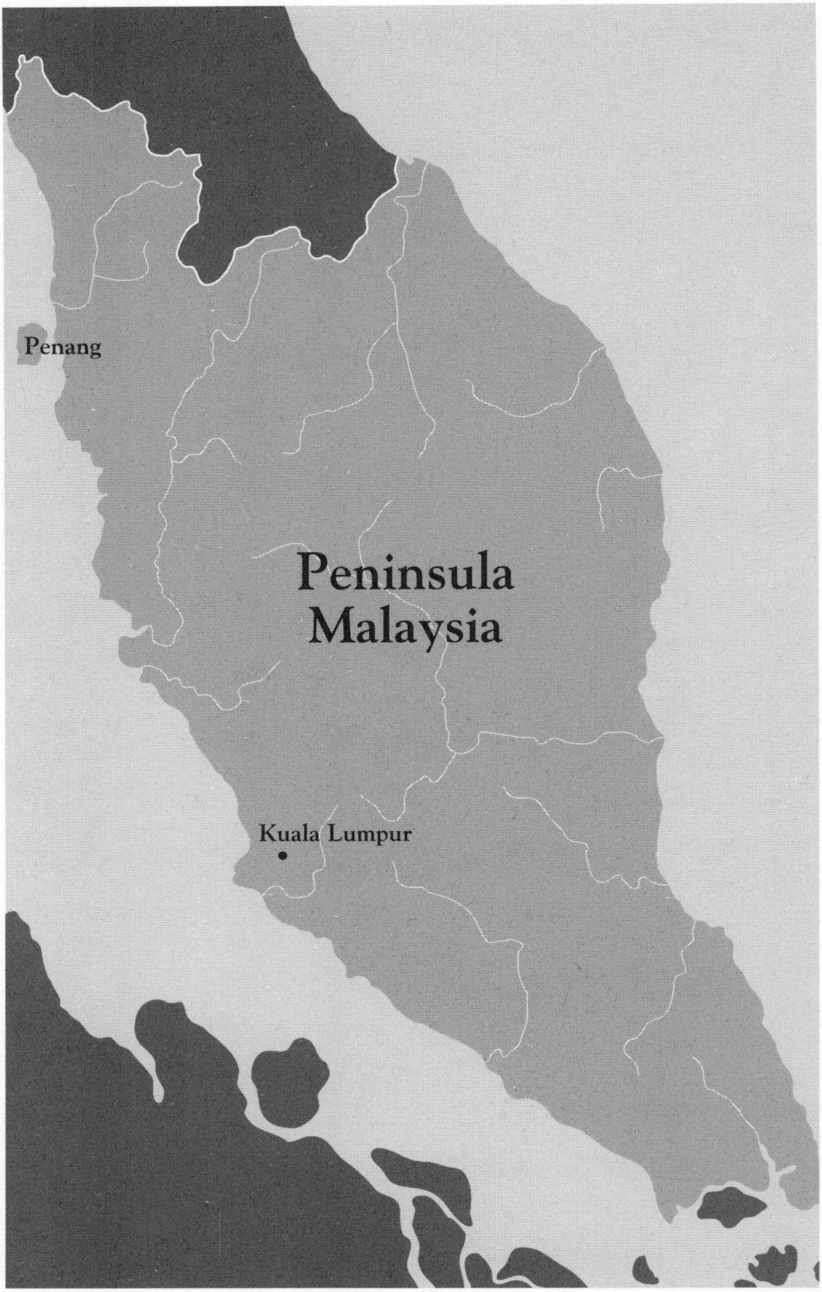

Penang

Peninsula Malaysia

Kuala Lumpur

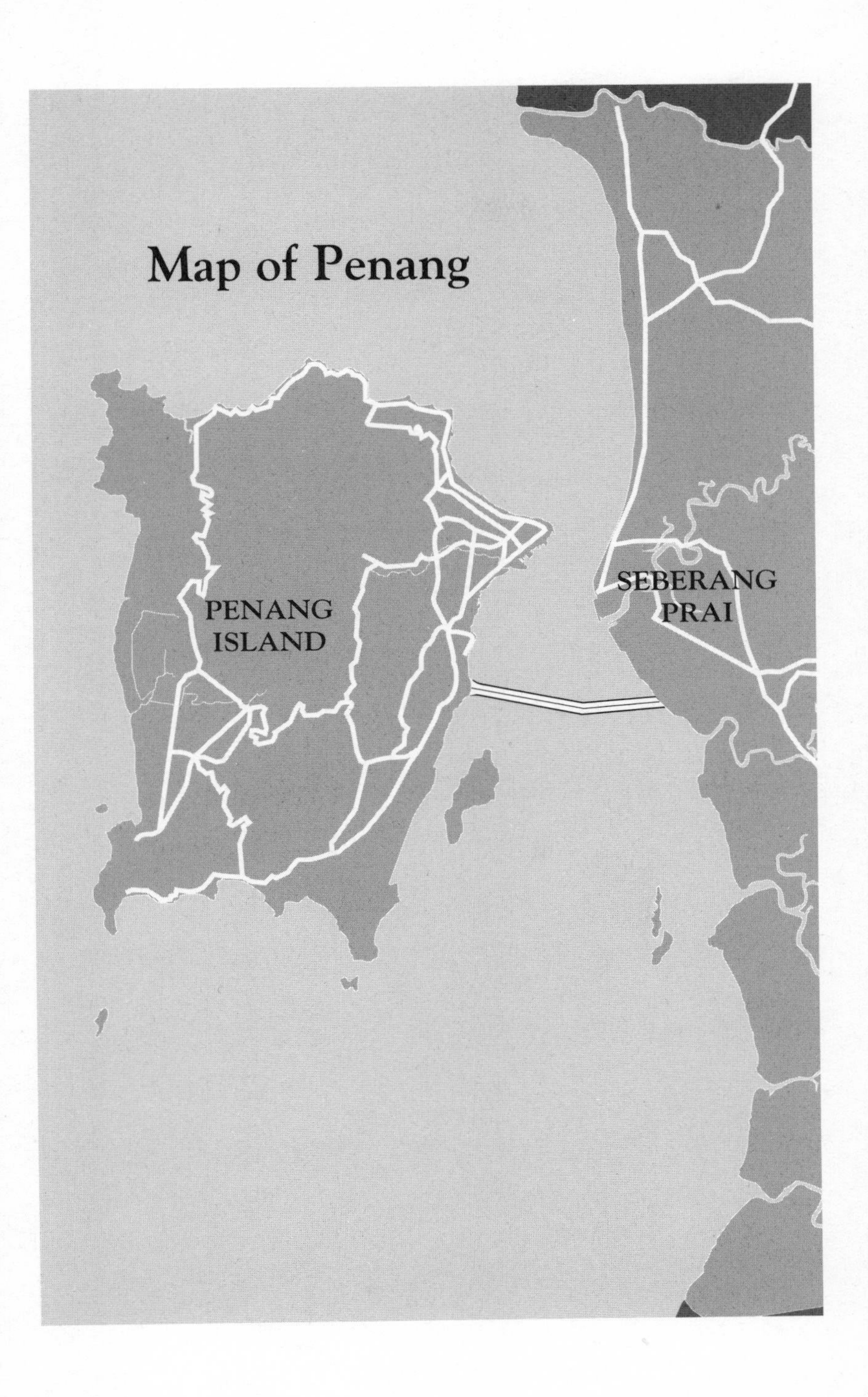

Map of Penang
PENANG ISLAND
SEBERANG PRAI

Part One

Penang: Its Story

1. The Foreigners' Rock

If you sit on the rocks at Batu Ferringhi, watching the hang-gliders soar overhead and water-skiers skim through the green surf, your thoughts may be filled with a pleasant sense of history. For apart from its natural beauty, this pile of primeval stones at the far end of Penang's northern beaches has always been a magnet for mariners.

Some lines of Francis Light's forbear may even slip into mind as you gaze out at the ocean: '*But who is this, what thing of sea or land... that so bedeck'd, ornate and gay, comes this way sailing like a stately ship of Tarsus, bound for th'isles of Javan or Gadier...*' True, such sentiments would hardly apply to the container ship on the horizon. But they conjure up a vision of one of the great sailing vessels of the past, converging on this rock which is the landmark of Penang. '*Sails fill'd, and streamers waving, courted by all the winds that hold them in play, an amber scent of odorous perfume her harbinger.*'

Yes, Milton's words seem appropriate here. Even the reference to a stately ship of Tarsus is not so far off the mark. Ten centuries before Christ, we are told, King Solomon chartered five seagoing vessels from Hiram, King of Tyre, and sent them off to the fabled land of Ophir. Three years later, they retuned bringing back a marvellous cargo of sandalwood, ebony, precious stones, gold, silver and ivory — to say nothing of monkeys and peacocks. The hieroglyphs at Deir-el-Bahri tell the story. 'Never were such things to any King since time was' state these Egyptian mural reliefs.

Ophir itself remains something of a myth. But given the length of time the trip took, and the haul the ships brought home, Josephus was probably correct in suggesting that its destination was Southeast Asia. Allowing for trade winds, three years would have been just about right for a voyage to these parts.

It is tempting to visualise King Solomon's ships anchored off the beach at Penang. Perhaps they put in here; for it seems likely that their destination was nearby Malacca, where the mountain still known as Mount Ophir contains prehistoric gold workings. And where, of course, monkeys and peacocks are common, and herds of wild elephants continue to come.

Be that as it may, the chances are that Egyptian and Phoenician traders visited Malaya during those last thousand years before Christ, very likely intermingling their blood, and perhaps erecting the stone monoliths of the Menhir and Dolmen types that are to be found here and there around the Southeast Asian countryside — and which, forming no part of any oriental tradition, remain an enigma.

Yet, it is apparent from the ancient Chinese writings that around 300 BC, Southeast Asia was populated by the *Kun-lun* or between-the-islands people: a significant term, since even before the time of Christ these folk called themselves the *Nusa Antara* — two Sanskrit words meaning exactly the same thing.

According to the Chinese, the *Nusa Antara* people had an advanced culture. They were adept at play-acting, music, the manufacture of painted cloth — that is, *batik* — and above all, in navigation. Their sailors took home from Canton and Tongking the knowledge of smelting and iron; it was they who first developed Southeast Asia's trade with China.

China, the world's largest and oldest homogenous block of human beings, stood then (as it has done until now) on the touch-line of non-Chinese affairs, neither interfering nor mingling, but occasionally recording what it saw. So to study the ethnic blend that forms the modern Malay race, we must turn to India.

By the 4th century BC, the Indo-Aryans of Central India already had trade links with Southeast Asia. In due course, Raja Chola, a king of the Gupta dynasty, sent frequent expeditions south in search of tin, ivory, spices, silk, cinnamon, sandalwood and other such goods — not only for local consumption, but also to be transported overland to the west (or by sea in Roman vessels from their trading port, Trivandrum, on India's southwest coast).

At that time Indo-Aryan India was spreading East in two almost concurrent movements, like the pincers of a crab. The left claw thrust out through Assam into northern Thailand, as well as Laos and Cambodia, where Indians founded a country known as Funan. The right claw came by sea to northern Sumatra, and thence to southern Thailand and the north of Malaya. Here they formed a state that straddled the Malayan peninsula, which was known as Langkasuka and included Penang.

Meanwhile Funan was consolidating its power: it became the greatest influence in art and religion in the whole of Southeast Asia, spreading a gentle and civilizing light from its capital, Angkor, through Java — one thinks of the vast Buddhist temple known as Borobudur near Djokjakarta — and eastwards as far as Bali.

For nearly a thousand years this influence prevailed. However, another entirely separate push occurred around the 9th century AD. This time, it was a commercial expansion by the Cholas from South India. Settling wherever they could trade, the Cholas added their Dravidian culture to the Malayan way of life.

But in the 13th century, much of the area was suddenly converted to Islam. For after the Moghuls had swept through India with the

Star and Crescent at the head of their horsemen, Indian merchants and seamen brought the Muslim religion to the Nusantara world. Marco Polo noted, on his return from China in 1292, that the ruler of Perlak in northeast Sumatra was already a Muslim.

Arab teachers from the Hadramaut also appeared. These enterprising Syed, Sheikh and other 'land-and-slave-owning' settlers grew to become the leaders of Southeast Asian society, intermarrying with the local people to form a ruling aristocracy, and introducing the strain of Arab blood that is so notable a characteristic among the chief Malay and Indonesian families.

Meanwhile China continued to stand impassively aside. If China had always exerted its power over those it considered to be its kith and kin (to the extent of actually ruling over Vietnam from 111 BC to 939 AD) it never had any protective or acquisitive interest in the great Nusantara regions of Malaya and Indonesia.

All the same, China was not aloof to trade, even with far away places. In 1408, the Ming Emperor Yung Lo instructed a Muslim eunuch of his court to produce charts of Southeast Asia, and to examine the trading possibilities with Africa. Elevated to the rank of Admiral, Ma Cheng Ho was given command of a fleet of 300 enormous junks.

These fantastic vessels were well over 200 feet (61 metres) in length, with a beam of more than 45 feet (13 metres). They carried a great press of canvas on five masts, and employed crews ranging up to 500 men in each ship. Each vessel had an entire in-between-deck given over to the rearing of pigs and the cultivation of vegetables as victuals for the officers and crew. Admiral Ma Cheng Ho made several successful voyages to Africa, during the course of which he called in regularly at Java, Malacca and Kedah.

To commemorate his visits, shrines and temples were erected by local Chinese populations, which indicate that Chinese citizens were already resident in Penang by the early years of the 15th century —

at the village of Batu Maung, to be precise. And there is no reason to doubt that small communities of Chinese had been quietly living on the shores of the island, carrying on their lives in their usual unostentatious yet profitable manner, for longer than anyone could say; for millennia, perhaps.

Now, having glanced briefly at the ethnical background, let us take up our story at the moment when these people received the first impact of a totally alien civilisation; that is, their first encounter with the West. It was to be an explosion that rocked forever the settled foundations of Southeast Asia, and gave a special identity to Penang.

2. The Europeans Arrive

The Portuguese lit the fuse, as it were. Having rounded the Cape of Good Hope, they first made a settlement at Goa. And while Alfonso de Sequeira sailed down the narrow seas between Sumatra and Malaya on his way to China, Albuquerque captured the famous trading port of Malacca.

If the arrival of the Portuguese caused an initial shock of surprise at the existence of these pale-faced 'White Bengalis', the people of Malacca seem to have been happy to acquire various improved weapons to replace their primitive cannon and poisoned arrows, together with a good deal more trade. And that was about all.

It was only when Spain — England's up-and-coming rival — became master of Portugal in 1580 that British thoughts turned to the Portuguese possessions out East. For now was the chance to pounce on the spice trade: that precious commodity that alone made the roast beef of old England palatable during the long winter months, when for lack of fodder most of the cattle had to be slaughtered. Spices, above all pepper, were the answer to Europe's most pressing need — and they all came from Southeast Asia. In the Malacca Strait, the focal point for all seaborne traffic to the West, lay the opportunity to win rich pickings in a brawl with the enemy.

It was known that the Portuguese landed regularly on the island of Penang, which was marked on their charts as 'Pulu Pinaom'. After the long haul across the Bay of Bengal, the secluded little anchorage at the north of the island was the first spot where a thirsty and exhausted crew could take on a supply of fresh water. Here a beautiful stream of clear mountain water flowed across the sand into a well-sheltered bay. It was marked by our rocky granite pile, which is still called Batu Ferringhi, or the 'Portuguese Rock'.

In English eyes, it was an ideal spot to lie hidden, and pounce on the enemy! With this plan in mind, a procession of three small square-rigged ships made their way out of Plymouth Harbour on an April morning in 1591. One of them was a shabby old vessel called the *Edward Bonaventure*, commanded by James Lancaster. Three years earlier, in the same ship, he had been one of Sir Francis Drake's captains who had harried the Spanish Armada up the English Channel to their destruction.

As it turned out, only the *Edward Bonaventure* succeeded in rounding the Cape of Good Hope and encountering the most dangerous and daunting waters in the world. Sixteen months after leaving England, with only 33 men and a boy left alive, the little ship came to anchor at Batu Ferringhi. On going ashore, Lancaster saw the tracks of some bare-footed people whose fires were still burning.

The next day, he relates, 'We espied a *canoa* which came neere to us, but would not come aboard us, having in it some 16 naked Indians, with whom, nevertheless, going afterwards on land, we had friendly conference and promise of victuals.' (These friendly folk were probably *Orang Laut*, a dark tribe of aquatic aborigines. They would not have been Malays, who are pale-skinned and, being Muslim, would not have gone about naked.)

While they were talking, three vessels appeared on the horizon. Whereupon, the *Edward Bonaventure* immediately gave chase, and captured a fine load of pepper from Perak. It was Lancaster's first taste of success, and from that time on the ship's hold began to fill.

Striking out from his base at Batu Ferringhi, he captured ship after ship until the *Bonaventure* was loaded so deep with loot that he had to leave Penang for fear of Portuguese reprisals. In the end James Lancaster never reached England with his spoil, for in the course of her long zigzag global voyage, the ship was taken over in the Caribbean by its mutinous crew (which did not do them much good; they were seized and butchered by the Spaniards at San Domingo). But he did manage to get home on a French vessel which took him aboard.

The expedition had ended in disaster. Yet Lancaster's abortive voyage to Penang had astonishing and far-reaching results, not the least of which was the emergence of England as a great imperial power.

For calling together his fellow navigators and a number of influential merchants, James Lancaster persuaded Queen Elizabeth to sanction the organisation of a Company which would alter the face of Asia. The name of the Company was officially 'The Governor and Merchants of London trading into the East Indies.' It was registered on 31 December 1600; its first director was Captain (now Sir James) Lancaster.

Although the East India Company (EIC) set up shop primarily to operate in Southeast Asia, subsequent events led the Honourable Company (as it chose to designate itself) to concentrate on trading between India and China.

For one thing, the Portuguese were firmly established in Macau and Malacca, while the Spanish had set themselves up in the Philippines. But more important, France and Holland were entering the game. For 90 years Portugal had kept the lucrative spice business largely to itself. Now the energy, greed and initiative of the West were to be concentrated in a power struggle for commercial supremacy in Southeast Asia.

It so happened that in the winter of 1580, a young Dutchman, hoping to learn Spanish and Portuguese, signed on as a clerk aboard the Portuguese vessel *San Salvador* bound for a three-year voyage to the East. The enticing story of what Jans Huygens van Linschoten saw and heard filled Holland's merchant adventurers with the desire to strike out East. As a result, the Dutch East India Company was also founded. In 1602 Admiral van Heemskerk sailed to Johor at the south of the Malay peninsula and made trade arrangements with the Ruler, leaving a certain *Mijnheer* Jacob Buisen there as Holland's first commercial representative. Four years later the Dutch soundly thrashed the Portuguese in a sea fight off Malacca. With the 'Portingals' now cornered, a head-on collision between the rival East India Companies was inevitable.

For a while, England and Holland came to an understanding by which England dug itself firmly into India, while Holland made a scoop in Southeast Asia (over which Britain no longer affected, after the manner of the fox and the sour grapes, to entertain much interest).

However, a third contender appeared on the scene, once again prompted by a literary composition. In the mid-17th century a brilliant and witty young French philosopher named Francois Bernier, who had been physician to the Moghul Emperor of India at Delhi, wrote a book on his travels and experiences. It was acclaimed throughout France, and read with fascination by Colbert, the chief minister of Louis XIV. So deep an impression did Bernier's chronicle make upon him of the riches and opportunities lying await in India for those with enterprise and courage that in 1664 Colbert caused a French East India Company to be set up as well.

By now the EIC, familiarly known as John Company, comfortably established at Fort William in Madras, was concerned chiefly with India and the tea trade between China and the London market. But while keeping a wary eye on these disturbing new competitors, and steering clear of the Dutch in Southeast Asia, it still had a sharp nose for the considerable country trade with these further Eastern waters.

This country trade consisted of a number of independent commercial concerns owned largely by British, Portuguese, Armenian and Indian shareholders who ran small locally-built brigs trading out of Indian ports in Southeast Asia. These vessels were licensed to undertake trade wherever they wished except China, at their own risk, of course. But with the obligation to make first offer of all their cargoes to the Company (who thus had hands clean as Pilate's to show Holland).

Many of these local coasters poked their bluff bows into Eastern waters, including those of Penang. One such independent trader was Captain Thomas Forrest, who left the first detailed account of the island.

Whatever may have been happening elsewhere, the little island of Penang had slumbered on. It was visited occasionally by Chinese fishermen from the mainland, who built a small temple on a northern headland known as *Tanjong Tokong* (The Headland of the Shrine) and a Chinese population lived in the village of Batu Maung on the southeast coast. But with so much trade running through the Malacca Strait, Penang had also become a convenient hideout for pirates. And whereas in former times a good number of Malays had lived along the coastline as fishermen and farmers, they now inhabited the island at their peril. The Sultan of Kedah, to whom Penang belonged, regarded these people as no more than criminals who had run away from the arm of the law, or from the system of taxation and feudal labour on which the country was organised. For a Malay to be caught on Penang meant death.

So it is not surprising that the island had once been much more populous than Captain Forrest found it during his visits between 1760 and 1780. Shortly before he first went ashore, the place must have suffered one of the periodic incursions by the Ruler of Kedah's armed forces, since he merely found the burnt-out remains of eight villages along the north coast, as well as an abandoned clearing on the east side of the central range of mountains, which is said to have been worked by one Dato Andor some 50 years previously. But Forrest also drew attention to Penang's wonderful drinking water, both from a waterfall in the eastern foothills as well as the stream near the little rock of Batu Ferringhi.

Yet what the old sea captain could not know as he wandered under the trees and beside the streams, was that this idyllic tropical island was about to become the springboard for a dominance by his countrymen that would do as much to awake the slumbering orient as any other action in history.

3. The Iconic Captain

Had Francis Light not been born out of wedlock and been baptised with the family's name of Negus, the course of events might have been quite different. He might have remained at Dallinghoo or achieved renown in England like his grandfather Francis Negus, a drinking companion of George II, and never founded the settlement at Penang. Conversely, Penang might now have a Negus Hotel with stirrup-cups to rival the Singapore Slings at Raffles.

Actually Light grew up in an affectionate home and was sent to the best school in the neighbourhood, to which he walked along the pleasant quaysides of the little Suffolk port of Woodbridge to the music of creaking blocks and tackle and the smell of rope and tar. And no doubt, during holidays, he was also to be found with a gang of equally barefooted companions running about the deck or swinging under the jib boom of any coastal brig that happened to be around.

With that background, it is not surprising to find him at eighteen, already signed on as a Cadet aboard one of His Majesty's elderly frigates called *HMS Captain*, from which he was promoted to Midshipman first to *HMS Dragon* and finally to the lumbering great ship-of-the-line *HMS Arrogant*. On convoy duty between Plymouth and Gibraltar, he made friends with a fellow Midshipman called James Scott. This large blond Scotsman, the younger brother of a muscular student at Edinburgh University nicknamed 'Beardy' Scott who was in time to become the grandfather of Sir Walter Scott, remained his lifelong colleague and made his own mark in Penang.

But in 1763, *HMS Arrogant* was laid up in mothballs on the signing of the Treaty of Paris, and the officers were discharge on six months' half pay. Whereupon James Scott left for India as a civilian, and a year later Francis Light followed in his footsteps, presumably responding to the lure of adventure.

Having arrived at Madras in June 1765, Light found himself in luck, for the old established shipping business known as Jourdain, Sullivan & de Souza, one of the concerns carrying on the country trade under license from John Company, was looking for a qualified young mariner.

Light was given command of the *Speedwell*, a handsome little brig (two masts, square-rigged on both) technically known as a Snow. In this handy ship with her well-trained Lascar crew, his job was to carry on the firm's business between Madras, Sumatra, and the west coast of the Malayan peninsula. J. S. & de Souza had already established a tenuous trade link with the Sultan of Acheen in northern Sumatra, where they shared the services of a Mr. Gowan Harrop, who represented the Association of Madras Merchants at Kota Raja, the Achineese capital. Francis Light was instructed to go there and give them a boost.

Meanwhile in Kedah, on the other side of the Malacca Strait, the old Sultan Mohamad Jiva was beset with problems.

He had permanent difficulties with his Ligor overlord concerning the question of tribute, which the Siamese expected to receive every three years. This took the form of a tree, constructed of gold and silver coins, named in Malay the *Pokok Mas dan Perak* or in English, the tree of gold and silver. In theory it merely perpetuated an age-long argument, traditionally held by the Kedah Malays, that this 'tree' was a brotherly gift from one free country to another to be granted or withheld at pleasure and certainly never to be demanded as of right (though tribute it certainly was).

Not only was there constant squabbling and bloodshed over the tribute affair with the infidel and the foreign power of Ligor — infidel because Kedah was Muslim, whereas the Ligor rulers were Buddhist — but worse trouble looked like brewing up between Kedah and a race of sea rovers from the Sula Sea. These Ulu or Bugis folk, denied their traditional livelihood as coastal traders by the arrival of the Dutch a hundred years previously, had turned into pirates. They had settled along the coastline just south of Kedah in the area known from ancient times as Selangor, and were becoming a menace throughout the Malacca Strait.

Yet worst of all, a domestic turmoil was raging in the court of Kedah. For as it happened, Sultan Mohamed Jiva, when nearing the age of 60 without a direct male heir to the throne, had appointed his nephew to succeed him after his death. And then suddenly, to the Sultan's surprise and delight, a slave girl or minor concubine bore him a son named Abdullah. The old monarch was so infatuated by this child that he promptly renounced the edict in favour of his nephew and appointed little Abdullah to succeed him as ruler. The next thing he knew was that civil war had broken out, led by his disappointed nephew and his outraged brothers, who called in the Bugis of Selangor for help.

Casting around to see where he could seek assistance in this awkward predicament, the Sultan immediately thought of England's EIC. If he could induce the English to come to his aid, it would solve all his problems, for not only would the civil uprising be quelled, but the menace of the Bugis and even the tribute affair with Ligor would be speedily resolved.

News travelled quickly in the East, and the Sultan soon heard about the presence in Acheen of Captain Francis Light. This young Englishman, he perceived, was precisely the person he needed to carry out the plan that was forming in his mind, namely, to offer the British a trading station in return for their protection.

The question was how to persuade Light to leave his base in Acheen and set up a trading station in Kedah. And at this point (we must assume) the wily old Sultan's attention focused on the seductive daughter of the Portuguese captain who ran his small fleet of *prahus*. Nubile, brunette, shapely and voluptuous, this clever girl who had been brought up at the Sultan's court and was now just back from her English education at a convent in Madras, would know how to entice a lonely, young English sea captain!

Mohamed Jiva's plan worked like a charm. Leaving aside conjectures, even the most conservative of Malayan historians accept as genuine the handwritten document dated 1772 and now in the British Museum archives, which states that Francis Light, who worked with Mr. Harrop in Acheen, came over to Kuala Kedah on the Malayan peninsula accompanied by a lady envoy from the Sultan of Kedah who had brought him an invitation from the Sultan of Kedah 'to set up a factory at that place.'

What is more, Francis Light's own will signed on his deathbed, indicates that he first took up with a lady named Martinha Rozells in 1772 (presumably an anglification of the Portuguese Rosales) and this was also the year in which both of them are recorded as setting up a factory or trading station at the Fort of Kuala Kedah in the name of Jordain, Sullivan & de Souza. It is worth noting, by the way, that 16 years later Captain Elisha Trapaud of the Madras Engineers, who by that time had become Light's second-in-command, published a book in London in which he gave details of the marriage ceremony of Francis Light 'according to Malay custom' to a lady of the Kedah court whom he describes as a 'Royal Princess'. The Sultan, he states, had 'bestowed on him a princess of his blood in marriage' as a reward to Light for 'quelling some troubles in his dominions.'

Here it should be noted that the Royal courts of Malaya have always been generous in taking the children of their friends and courtiers into the royal entourage, and the term Royal Princess should be taken in its polite connotation, quite normal in old-fashioned Malay courtesy, as distinguished lady of the court. But without going so far as to suggest that Martinha may have been a half-sister to the young Abdullah, it does seem abundantly clear that she and the Lady Envoy were one and the same person.

Be that as it may, some weeks elapsed before the young skipper and the Lady Envoy returned, loaded with suitable presents for the Sultan. For Francis Light was only too eager to establish a commercial foothold at Kuala Kedah. On their arrival, they found Mohamed Jiva up north, his capital at Alor Star having been burnt by the Bugis. At this point Light may very well have made himself useful, for in August 1777 he reported to his principals in Madras that the Sultan had offered his seaport, and indeed the whole coastline up to Penang, in return for help against Selangor, and that he was prepared to share his trade monopoly with the British. There were all the makings, Light told them, for a most satisfactory agreement.

Since military aid was quite beyond the scope of a mere trading firm, the East India Company decided to send a mission of its own. It needed a port of call somewhere in the Malayan archipelago where its ships could harbour and refit while waiting for favourable winds (for the monsoons controlled the timing of voyages). If the trade prospects at Kedah were as tempting as Light seemed to think, the company was quite prepared to elbow him out and pounce on the concession itself. There was also the attraction of possessing a potential naval base on the eastern side of the Bay of Bengal.

A young official was therefore dispatched to Kedah, only to find that the Sultan's demands for an offensive alliance went beyond his terms of reference. And unfortunately, the hesitant and dandified figure of the Hon. Edward Monkton (accompanied by his inevitable Portuguese interpreter, Mr. de Mello) was no match against local intrigues. In fact, so badly did he bungle the negotiations that the Sultan wrote a stinging note to the Governor-General enquiring whether they had no one better to send him than a 'stuttering jackanapes of a boy'. Though Light, who was forced to remain a passive observer, did his utmost to retrieve the situation, and even helped secure a draft treaty, the mission failed when it became clear that the Company's support would not include aid against Selangor. Things might have turned out differently had negotiations been left to the man on the spot; instead Light was castigated by the Madras Council for having been the author of a fiasco.

'The offer the Sultan made me on my first arrival I thought so advantageous that not to have accepted it seemed downright folly,' he complained on 1 June 1772 to Warren Hastings. But Hastings was too preoccupied turning the Company's possessions in India into an empire to have much time for the trade or politics of Malaya.

For Francis and Martinha, it was a devastating blow. Had Monkton been more accommodating over the matter of armaments instead of riling the Sultan with his bad manners, the old man would have been prepared, as he had already stated in writing, to 'make over to Captain Light all the lands, including the island of Pulau Pinang, from Kuala Kedah down to the Krian River.' Instead of which Light had been made to lose face in Kedah and suffer disgrace in Madras. With his private trade in ruins, the only thing to do was sail off aboard the *Speedwell* to the island of Ujong Salang, now known as Phuket, and join forces with his old shipmate, James Scott, who had set himself up as an independent trader there.

Sailing far and wide in the Eastern seas, Light built up a considerable trading business in partnership with Scott. Indeed he became such a notable local figure that the King of Siam summoned him to Ayudhia and invested him with the proud title of Chao Phya (which means Lord Lieutenant) of the Island of Phuket. And during the 11 years that this was his home, Light got to know the Malayan waters so well that he compiled a mariner's guidebook describing every port in the archipelago.

Yet all along, by letter or whenever they were in Calcutta, he and Scott continued to insist on the need for a British port as a magazine of trade on the east side of the Bay of Bengal. Understandably they stressed the advantages of Phuket, whereas Thomas Forrest, who was now commanding John Company's Marine at Bencoolen, took up the argument in favour of Penang. And then an event happened to give urgency to the project.

The French established themselves at Trincomalee in Ceylon, and in 1783 Admiral le Baille blockaded Calcutta. (He also captured Francis Light, who was cruising off the Caromandal coast in his small schooner *Blake*, along with that engaging raconteur and wit, William Hickey).

Light was able to escape during a moment of thick fog, and when he returned to Phuket, James Scott had exciting news. This was that Warren Hastings had spoken in council about the 'absolute necessity of obtaining a port on the east side of the Bay of Bengal.'

The two old shipmates went to work. Scott wrote to Hastings recommending his friend for any forthcoming negotiations concerning Penang while Light himself, who had long since resumed trading with Kedah and was on good terms with the new young Sultan, boldly took the initiative of asking Abdullah for the island of Penang in return for British protection. On 13 February 1786 he was able to tell the acting Governor-General that: 'I have made use of the interest and influence I have with the King of Kedah to secure a grant of the Island of Penang to the Honourable Company. The King of Kedah who now solicits your friendship and allegiance, has sent me a grant of the Island of Penang and has also annexed to the Grant some requests.'

It was a curious reversal of the previous negotiations, for Light was appointed Abdullah's *wakil* or representative, to deal with the Company in Calcutta. The Sultan's demands were clear: he sought protection from his enemies and a compensation of 30,000 Spanish dollars a year for the loss of trade — a high sum that Light considered to be highly negotiable.

Though nothing much had changed, the Council (after paying him a corporate tribute which made some amends for its previous censure) appointed the Sultan's *wakil* as head of the mission to occupy Penang. But instead of a formal agreement to Abdullah's terms, Light was given a vague undertaking that the Company would station a vessel at Penang and 'take care that the king of Kedah shall not be a sufferer by an English settlement being formed on the island of Penang.'

The fulfilment of his dream was in sight. Yet the sailor empire-builder would have to sail very close to the wind to pull it off.

4. Hoisting The Flag

A few weeks later three small vessels made their way down the lower reaches of the Hoogly and out into the Bay of Bengal. First came Captain Light aboard his new flagship *Eliza*, whilst to port and starboard the *Prince Henry* and his own *Speedwell* surged behind in the morning breeze. On board the little fleet were 100 newly-raised Native marines, 30 lascars and 15 artillery men under the command of Captain Elisha Trapaud, and five other British officers.

In his cabin, Light sat in shirtsleeves, his high-collared blue reefer jacket with its gold gorgettes hanging over a chair, as he watched his secretary Thomas Pigou tally up the 30,000 rupees that the Select Committee at Calcutta had granted as expenses for the expedition.

The newly appointed Superintendent was pondering over his instructions ('The success of this important undertaking depends entirely on the good conduct of the Conductor, especially during its infant state.') and in particular the letter he was to deliver to the Sultan.

'Your friendly letter containing a Grant of Pulau Pinang to the Company' Sir John Macpherson, the acting Governor-General, had written to Sultan Abdullah, 'was delivered to me by Captain Light on 16 February 1786. Captain Light has also made known to me the requests of my friend and brother, which having heard, we have already transmitted to the Honourable English Company. I have also ordered a ship of war to the defence of the island and the protection of the coast of Kedah.'

Fine words. But would they be convincing enough to satisfy the Sultan and enable him to conclude an agreement satisfactory to both sides?

His thoughts turned to Martinha and their daughter Sarah. Both had gone back to Kuala Kedah to stay with Martinha's sister Yeen, for the birth of their next child. The baby boy who had been born on the eve of the foundation of a settlement in Penang was to be called William after Francis Light's father. (And though nobody could foresee it, would one day himself found the city of Adelaide.) All three were waiting for him at the Sultan's court in Kedah.

The merchants at Kuala Kedah were in the hands of a local strongman, 'a dark, cunning, villainous black Chulla' as Light described him, now endowed with the high title of Dato Sri Raja, though he had formerly been a mere coolie named Jamual, 'who has engrossed the whole of the administration.' On the pretext of saving the Sultan from assassination, this upstart had locked Abdullah up in a brick fort, and was playing 'both ends against the middle' — the Chulla community on one side, the Sultan on the other — and manipulating both from a central position.

Yet while ostensibly siding with his brother Chulla merchants, Jamual was secretly intending that, after striking the hardest bargain that he could drive, Light should gain possession of Penang. In this Jamual was actuated by no love of the English, but by the fact that he had accumulated a vast ill-gotten fortune and was hated by everybody. Jamual reckoned that the Sultan's life was unlikely to be a long one (for a variety of reasons) and once Abdullah was gone, his own riches, to say nothing of his life, would be at risk. He needed to find a place where both his life and his fortune would be under safe protection and in the hands of the East India Company, Penang would provide an ideal shelter.

So the unedifying situation that greeted Light was that of the Chief Minister playing his own game, while the Chulla business community was up in arms at his reappearance with some foreign scheme they mistrusted; and the Sultan Abdullah, whose signature was necessary for every move, was chafing away virtually alone in his well-guarded fort up-river, with nobody to give him good advice.

Moreover, as the apprehensive Portuguese court officials and their families were aware, an even greater menace was impending. Four years previously, Captain Coston together with all his officers — that is to say, every man aboard who had as white a skin as they had themselves — had been brutally murdered by a party of Malays from Kedah whilst their sloop *Friendship* was lying at anchor in the lea of the Langkawi islands. And once more the Malay community, now buzzing like a hornet's nest, was liable at any moment to allow their hatreds to overflow and run amok. If it came to real trouble, the local Portuguese feared that they would be the victims, together with Light and his crew as well as any Chinese or Chulla to whom the Malays owed money.

It was a delicate situation that only a man with Light's experience of Asia could have handled, as he did, with patience, intuition, and in the end, decisive action.

By the evening of 8 July after prolonged negotiations, the Sultan and Francis Light reached a tentative agreement, the basis of which was that provided arms and ammunition were supplied to the Sultan by the East India Company, a settlement might be created on the island of Penang. There and then, Light agreed to hand over as many firearms and ammunition as he could spare, apparently confident that Calcutta would go along with the general terms of the bargain he had struck; and proposed to move into

Penang without further delay. But at the last moment both the Sultan and Jamual demurred, saying in effect 'not until we have the arms and ammunition.'

At this point Light, conscious of the explosive situation ashore and of his own responsibility for the success of the undertaking, merely rowed off down-river in the pouring rain and boarded the *Eliza* with the tentative agreement in his pocket. Whereby a mark of interrogation has hung over his integrity ever since.

Having delivered the arms and ammunition he had promised, Light waited on events; and what happened during the next two days prompted him to make up his mind about what to do next.

For on 13 July a positive stampede to the shoreline broke out among Kuala Kedah's non-Muslim population. The Portuguese, along with a large number of Chinese, appeared to be making a wholesale getaway, with chickens and ducks, baggage and goods. Paddling out in every form of float and raft, they poured aboard the little British fleet.

Still Francis Light remained at anchor, painfully aware of the dilemma that faced him. Should he wait for the agreement to be ratified by Calcutta as the Sultan demanded, or head for Penang immediately? A reply from Calcutta would take weeks; yet the need for Penang as a port and an arsenal was vital and urgent. The whole object of the expedition was to conclude the matter with all speed; he knew that the Sultan was also in touch with the Dutch and might change his mind overnight.

Yet it was not until two priests from the local Catholic church (a recent extension of the Catholic Mission to Siam) appeared on board accompanied by Martinha and the children that he at last took his decision. "We are being massacred," they told him, "All the Christians will be massacred if they stay on a day longer. Jamual has been collecting *prahus* to attack you tonight and sack all three of your ships."

Whether this information was true or not, it confirmed his own suspicion that mischief was afoot, and prompted him into immediate action. "Very well," he said to his officers, "If that's the way they want it, so it shall be. We will get weigh anchor at 6 pm."

That evening, the three overcrowded vessels sailed for Penang and anchored north of the present Esplanade of George Town on Monday 15 July 1786 at 5 pm.

In thus jumping the gun, Light amazed the Kedah leaders. He had done two things beyond their comprehension. He had taken independent action, and apparently accepted personal responsibility for it — both rare and reprehensible failings by the traditional Malay way of thinking. The fact that he had not left the decision in the hands of the authorities in Calcutta, so that the game of political bargaining could go on for months and he could escape blame (even if the delay ruined Britain's commerce in Southeast Asia) but instead dashed in regardless, showed him to be a masterful and therefore a highly dangerous person. In the light of this disclosure the whole stance of the Kedah government would have to be reconsidered. As Light had so clearly shown himself to be a man of action, it might be best to deal with the matter in a conciliatory fashion, at least at first. (It is possible, of course, that Dato Jamual was feigning astonishment, having engineered events to scare Light into action). So the authorities in Kedah merely contented themselves by sending two observers to Penang to report on what was happening.

The reaction of the Malay peasantry on the island was quite different, and from the point of view of these observers most disturbing. For one thing, the headman of the three tiny Malay communities who had been hiding at Batu Gantong, Bukit Dunbar and Bayan Lepas — totalling 49 souls — approached Light asking for permission to come out of concealment if he would protect them from the Sultan of Kedah; in return for which they would gladly work for him. Light was happy to agree to their request, and gave them an area in which to build their homes that has been known ever since as Malay Street. The 49 Malays rejoiced even further when he actually offered them payment at the rate of one Spanish dollar or *doubloon* for every hundred trunks of a hard palm tree known as a *nibong* that they might care to fell, trim and bring out of the jungle into camp. Since a Spanish dollar was worth more than a month's salary to a working man, this was perhaps the first time they had ever had the chance to earn real money in their lives.

But the observers reported that Light was taking on serfs and criminals and urging them to defy the Sultan. If he were allowed to settle down in Penang with such inflammable new ideas, he would become a menace to the whole traditional Malay system of government.

Even more disquieting, from their point of view, was the reaction of the Chinese. The morning after the little fleet anchored off Penang the headman or Kapitan China, of a village on the mainland just off the island, put in an appearance before Francis Light. This man, Khoh Lee Wan, had sailed across in two large *sampans*, one in which to return to Kedah and the other, loaded to the gunwales with a cargo of fresh fish, to leave behind. Having greeted Light politely from his boat, Khoh Lee Wan explained that the second *sampan*, together with its cargo of fish, the net and the two fishermen, were by way of a slight gift from him to the Commander, who was sure to be needing fresh fish daily for himself and his crews.

After these had been received with gratitude, Khoh Lee Wan enquired whether it would be acceptable if he and his family should decide to take up residence on the island. Light immediately agreed, with the result that within a week no less than 60 Chinese families, totalling some 600 people, were busily employed in Penang building their homes along what is still called China Street.

One is bound to sympathise with the watching Malay chiefs, representing the ruling hierarchy of the ancient race, as these scenes were enacted before them. It must have seemed as though the entire structure of feudal Malaya was crumbling before their eyes.

Meanwhile the newcomers from the ships to say nothing of the Reverend Fathers Garnault and Coudé — crossing themselves as they knelt on the sands of their new home — were actively settling in. The Marines swam and larked as they chopped saplings to serve as framework for huts made of pandanus-leaf matting brought from Calcutta. But when it came to clearing the end of the sandy point that is today the site of George Town, they were less cooperative, complaining that the dense covering of Panaga trees was so bad that their coils doubled up like pieces of lead. In the end a ship was sent to Malacca to buy some native axe-heads; but while she was away, Light resorted to ruse. Loading a cannon with coins, he fired it periodically off into the undergrowth. There was no complaint of inactivity after that.

During this time, he imperceptibly changed from Commander of the *Eliza* into Superintendent of Penang, controlling activities from an administrative tent. As the Malays brought in the palm trunks, he paced out the line of a fence to demarcate the official area, and this primitive stockade, later built over with brick by a subsequent Governor, is the original lay-out of the present Fort Cornwallis.

A well was dug at the head of a track that ran westwards from the Point, and by common consent this first road was immediately called Light Street. Blacksmiths, sail makers and 'chippies' erected their palm-thatch stalls along both sides of it, while the Catholic fathers started building a Church and a school. The officers set up their own mess, where they could foregather after gruelling days spent unloading stowage, and supervising stowage and accommodation.

But as he sat in his tent in the midst of this busy scene — arranging for a thatched wooden house to be built for Martinha and the children a little way along the foreshore, listening to complaints and making decisions, Light's mind was in a quandary.

He had to decide whether to take formal possession of the island. And this depended on whether Calcutta ratified the agreement he had made with the Sultan to supply arms and ammunition. What would happen if John Company failed to do so and the Sultan refused them permission to remain at Penang, as he very well might?

Light knew that he had gone too far now for any withdrawal to be considered. Chinese and Malays had already come under his promise of protection, and he could not let them down. Moreover both the Company and the Navy had urgent need of Penang. Surely his duty was clear?

Finally, 27 days after the landing, two East Indiamen appeared on the horizon. The Company vessels *Valentine* and *Vansittart* had come to pay their respects to the new Settlement and offer any assistance that might be needed.

If they carried the Governor-General's ratification of his agreement with the Sultan, then all would be well. But even if they didn't, he was still morally bound to go ahead. Calcutta would wash its hands off him if things went wrong, and take all the credit if they went right. Whatever happened, he was sure to be blamed.

Unhappily the ships brought no letters.

Very well then, Light sent a signal to the ships' commanders requesting their company ashore that evening. With the result, as he noted in his diary, that 'On Sunday 11 August 1786 Captains Wall and Lewin came ashore with several passengers. Saluted them with nine guns. Thought this the most favourable opportunity for taking possession of the island.'

To mark this unilateral declaration of possession, the small group of sailors and merchants, all dressed in their Sunday best in this first dawn of Britain's Southeast Asian commercial adventure, clustered bare-headed around a tall gallant mast lashed to a tree trunk, and in the noonday breeze under the enormous Asian sky, heard Francis Light, hat in hand, read out the following proclamation:

> *These are to certify that agreeable to my orders and instructions from the Honourable Governor-General and Council of Bengal, I have this day taken possession of this island called Pooloo Pinang now named Prince of Wales Island and hoisted the British colours in the name of His Majesty George the Third and for the use of the East India Company, this eleventh day of August 1786, being the eve of the Prince of Wales' birthday.*

The officers and guests hauled together as the Colours went up. And as the guns fired a Royal salute and the Marines three volleys, Elisha Trapaud dashed off a sketch of the scene to send to his mother.

The fact that Britain's possession of Penang hinged solely on the supply of arms and ammunition to the Sultan of Kedah was quietly overlooked. It was an omission that was to cause no little trouble in time to come.

5. A Less Than Gentle Persuasion

Penang was ideal for its job. The island had everything that was needed; a perfect strategic and mercantile position, a well-sheltered deepwater harbour, flat land beside the sea for a settlement, good timber for ship-building, and best of all, abundant sparkling-clear drinking water for ships and settlers.

It was a lovely place, too. When relaxing from the endless grind of supervising the little town take shape, Light's happiest retreat was the hilly centre of his new domain — an enchanting, jungle-covered hinterland rising to nearly three thousand feet, with silent valleys and clear streams full of fish, where sunbeams danced on ferns and amaryllis. From here, he could gaze down at the sea far below, ruffled by the monsoon and glimpsed through the gaps in the low clouds, those 'charmed magic casements opening on the foam of perilous seas in fairyland forlorn.'

One of the first things he did after clearing the Point (or *Tanjong* as the Malays call it) was to have a way cut to the very top of the hill. The path he made was, and still is, a winding packhorse trail leading over six miles from the waterfall to a hilltop plateau 2,500 feet (762 metres) above the sea, which Light named the Macpherson Track in honour of the man who had appointed him Superintendent.

On this high plateau, Light cleared a patch of land and built a small bungalow. As a good Suffolk man he had said long ago that he would never be content until he had found a tropical island where he could grow strawberries. Now at last he had found it. Strawberry roots were brought out from Dallinghoo, and grew so well in his garden that the area became known as Strawberry Hill.

Within a few months of founding the Settlement, Light was joined by his partner James Scott, who also soon built himself a hill-house on a spur overlooking the town, which he described as 'The Highlands of Scotland'.

From his cool eyrie Francis Light could look down on the little town that was taking shape on the easternmost point of the island. He could see his own bungalow on the seashore a few hundred yards from the Fort with its growing stockade. He could also observe the clearing where the Reverend fathers were building their small thatched church and infant school — now the site of the catholic Cathedral of the Assumption, with beside it that tiny school's lineal descendant, St. Xavier's Institute, the oldest and most famous teaching establishment in all Malaysia.

Shops were opening; more and more ships were sailing in, George Town was beginning to come alive. Two years after its founding, some 5,000 people were pullulating like ants in the huddled huts and godowns along the thronging alleys, avidly buying and selling in their newly-found freedom under the British flag.

But what a tough job it had turned out to be! The flat land around the cantonment, being swampy, had required extensive drainage. It had been necessary to clear large tracts of jungle to create space for the rapid influx of settlers, and make roads. (Today's town planners will note, with a professional eye, that the network of roads which Light laid out still forms the ground plan of the city.)

These thoroughfares were now lined with bungalows built of timber with palm-thatched roofs, raised Malay-style on posts for protection against flooding — though not, unhappily, against fire. There had been emergencies such as a blaze that destroyed much of the bazaars; and above all, the need to maintain law and order — a serious problem from the start, for the rush to the Settlement had attracted some pretty unruly characters.

However these were the least of his troubles. The most constant worry of all was Kedah. Britain's possession of Penang depended on the Sultan being defended from his country's enemies; without that Abdullah would never have offered him the island in the first place. Light had written repeatedly to Calcutta for confirmation of this responsibility. But all he ever got in reply were instructions that he should 'use the influence of the Company for the security of the Sultan of Kedah' (whatever that might mean) while cautioning that the Company declined to become involved in military operations 'arising from quarrels between any of the Eastern princes.'

By 1790 the matter had reached a dangerous impasse. Having lost patience with such evasive quibbling, the Sultan was busy negotiating with the French at Pondicherry and the Dutch at Malacca. Unavailingly, he offered Penang to either of them if they would throw the English out and give him better terms.

Finally, in desperation, Kedah formed a Grand Alliance with Selangor, Trengganu, Johore, Lingga — and even Sumatran Siak and the distant Celebes, noted for their lanoon sea-fighters — to rid the Malayan peninsula of both Dutch and English. By December that year Light found it necessary to write urgently to Fort Williams reporting that two large war *prahus* from Mindanao in the Philippines and 25 supporting vessels from other places had attacked Malacca, and were gathering in strength off the mainland opposite Penang. Food supplies from Kedah, on which the island still largely depended, had been completely cut off, and all the villages along the adjacent coast had been forcibly evacuated and destroyed.

On receipt of this news, Calcutta bestirred itself sufficiently to send down *HMS Crown* with three companies of Sepoys. By the time they arrived an argument about money had broken out among the opposing forces, who dispersed towards the north apparently intent on having it out with the Siamese.

Nevertheless, the situation remained perilous. Francis Light did his best to arm and man three small 'cruizers' and also commandeered an armed ketch that happened to be lying at anchor in the roads. But when *Crown* arrived these fell out of his control, whereupon the ketch hurriedly left Penang to continue her voyage. Some days later *Crown* also sailed from Penang, with the result that the other merchant vessels in the harbour suddenly found it convenient to announce their departure also, leaving only the staunch (or possibly disabled) *Bombay Castle* in port.

Before long an army from Kedah once again appeared on the mainland coast and grew in strength until by the middle of March 1791, it numbered over ten thousand well-armed men. At this point Light wrote to the Sultan advising him to disband his troops immediately to avoid unnecessary bloodshed, 'which would be quite unavailing' he added. At the same time, to make things easier, he offered Abdullah an outright gift of 10,000 Spanish dollars. Though parleys continued for almost a month, the Sultan finally sent a letter which could only be read as an unequivocal declaration of war.

Across the still waters of the channel, Light could see the shoreline seething with tough fighting men, while behind them ranged a series of stockaded fortresses well supplied with heavy cannon. All this was clearly visible by spyglass from the waterfront of George Town. To seaward lay a long line of war-*prahus*, their glittering brass pieces ready-loaded along the gunwales. They were waiting for the order to strike at Penang.

At Light's disposal were 400 Sepoys under Captain Glass who had been left behind by *HMS Crown* and three small gunboats manned by amateur gunners and commanded by two Naval cadets. But he had no doubt what to do. 'Attack at once,' he ordered. And Captain Glass agreed with him.

Towed in barges by the cruizers under cover of darkness, Glass and his Sepoys made a successful landing on the mainland coast. In a concerted dash, they attacked the nearest fortress. Once secured, they turned its guns on the enemy's next fortress. This captured, they continued the process from fortress to fortress with such devastating effect that after seven days the Sultan sent an emissary to Penang with a message suing for peace.

Francis Light accepted the capitulation immediately, and offered to pay 6,000 Spanish dollars annually in settlement of all Kedah's claims in respect of the island of Penang for so long as the British remained there. At long last, that fundamental point had been settled. Agreement had been reached for Britain's possession of the island.

From John Company's point of view, their supervisor's bold and decisive action had paid heavy dividends. There was no more talk of military assistance, and the Treaty accepted by the chastened Sultan was quickly ratified by the Bengal government, which finally gave legal sanction to the acquisition of Penang. 'Force had succeeded where evasive diplomacy had failed, and force had cost a mere trifle' comments the historian Winstedt. One wonders what Light felt about it all before he died.

Indeed one does. At Penang itself, everything was going ahead better than he could have hoped; the Settlement was surging ahead like a brig with the wind in its sails. By 1792 George Town's population had already doubled to over ten thousand inhabitants, not counting 'strangers belonging to ships and *prahus* to a number between 1,500 and 2,000' which gave a clear indication of the volume of trade that was pouring through the port. By then over 250 well-built houses clustered along what were already known as Beach Street and Penang Street intersected at right angles by Light Street, China Street and Malay Street. Though many were still constructed of wood with palm thatch roofing, some had already been built with bricks and tiles. The Public Well in Light Street was in constant use. Out in the surrounding countryside, some 2,500 acres of land were under cultivation and producing over 400 tons of rice, with hopes of doubling that crop in the following year. Fruit trees, pepper, gambier and sugarcane were flourishing everywhere.

Now there were roads leading out of George Town like the fingers of an outspread hand. The longest of these cut straight through the jungle to the waterfall four miles to the west — where the Macpherson track began to wind up the hill — and along this muddy jungle highway, long caravans of buffalo-drawn water carts brought water to the visiting East Indiamen.

It seemed a cheerful and prosperous picture. But the English still had a hard lesson to learn. For malaria, the greatest killer of the East, was about to take a toll that would brand Penang for all its haunting beauty as the White Man's Grave.

No one understood malaria. If the low-lying marshy land was known to be dangerous, it was thought that was due to some noxious gas or miasma that seeped out of the rotting vegetation at night and caused men's death. Malaria was not associated with the presence of stagnant pools; certainly never with mosquitoes.

The houses up Strawberry Hill were considered healthy, and it was thought reasonably safe to live in town. But those with homes out in the clearing mysteriously began to sicken. Malays, crouching over their smudgy fires below the slatted bamboo floors of their rickety huts, seemed comparatively free from the fever; nor were the Chinese, crowded together in George Town and burning their perpetual joss-sticks in incense-filled rooms much affected by it. Yet the English, in their elegant garden houses with wide-open windows giving out on gardens full of tropical blooms, caught a fever and died.

Even an old-timer like Light was at risk.

It was part of his engagement with the Company as Superintendent of Penang that, being a trader by profession, he should support himself by his own commercial endeavours. He was merely given an allowance by Fort William to cover out-of-pocket expenses on official duty. There was nothing surprising about this, for Company officers were expected to do business for their own account, and many of them feathered their nests most lavishly.

But Light was far in advance of his time. Not only did he insist on a special clause being put into the articles of association before going back into business with his old partner James Scott in Penang to the effect that he 'would not interfere in the management', but in 1790 he wrote to the new Governor-General pointing out the invidious position in which he was placed. 'My expenses have amounted monthly to 1,500 dollars including buildings,' he explained to Lord Cornwallis 'and I know not of one emolument pertaining to this office except the influence in having first purchase of any commodity which comes into this port. This power, though never exacted by me, is supposed to be done, and occasions many malicious reports, with much uneasiness and vexations to myself. It is not what I do, but what may be done when the weight of office is made to act with the merchant. These apprehensions will continue to predominate so long as the Superintendent had it in his power to be the chief trader. My petition is, therefore, to your Lordship that you would not only free me from these accusations, but deprive me of the power of deserving them, by such increase in salary as will support the office with decency and enable me to make a small provision for an approaching old age.'

But unfortunately Lord Cornwallis was too busy raking in a fortune for himself to be moved by the justice of such an honest appeal, and merely replied that he 'refused to charge the revenues of Bengal with any extra burden' (which was rich coming from the man who was the heaviest extra burden himself).

Light therefore began to spend more time trying to improve his own properties. Two miles out of town he had acquired, in his own name, a somewhat marshy plantation in an area known as Telok Ayer Rajah. In addition he had begun to develop another plantation to the southwest which he called Suffolk and here he began to suffer from the hot flushes, cold shivers, and appalling headaches of the fever.

It was now that he decided it was time to send his six-year-old son William to England, where he had arranged with his old friend George Doughty, squire of Theberton near Melton, to take charge of the child's upbringing. Captain Lewin, who was in command of the vessel *Vansittart* agreed to take the lad back to London, and we can almost see the small boy clutching the skipper's large hand at the ship's gangway and struggling to fight down his tears, while his father told the skipper that the child had 'that sort of obstinacy that will not easily bend to harsh control.' The small boy, as we shall see later, was to be prominent in Australia's history.

Meanwhile, in the midst of his ill-health, Light was faced with a new anxiety; the news that France and England were again at war. Indeed his last great effort was directed towards preparing Penang against almost certain attacks from the French fleet.

Of defences there were none; the small fortified stockade was in ruins, whilst in Mauritius, then known as Ile de France, the French were busy fitting out an expedition to capture the Eastern trade. Light was writing desperately to Calcutta that 'the stockade has burst out in several places, gabions entirely rotten and the ramparts falling down, platforms quite decayed and not capable of bearing guns.' In the end he was forced to go ahead without the Company's approval and sanction the spending of 5,790 Spanish dollars for repairs to the Fortress — a sum Fort William eventually passed after much grumbling, 'though not' they hastened to add 'with our approbation.'

Although the French Admiral Sercy did indeed take command of a fleet to capture Penang, and might have done so had he not had the misfortune to run across the bows of *HMS Arrogant* and *Victorious* two days away from his destination and been given a good pummelling, that stage in the story of Penang was not reached until shortly after the death of its Founder.

Poor Light had struggled towards his inevitable end. After nearly 30 years in the East he was now yearning to go home, and was even making arrangements to buy a farm in his beloved Suffolk. 'I have a longing desire to become the owner of Golsberry Farm,' he wrote to George Doughty, 'Yet I have an inward sensation that though I may linger a year or two I conjecture that I shall not have the happiness to see you' and added as his last words, 'to plough your fields is a thousand times preferable to governing.'

An epitaph to ambition! Francis Light, a descendant of Milton and a kinsman of Marlborough, the first great British pioneer in Malaya who paved the way for all the others, died at Penang in the morning of 21 October 1794, and with him ended the initial chapter of Penang's entry into the strategy and politics of the western world.

6. Presidential Status

They say that it is still possible to find a joke about the Scots that was not dreamt up in Aberdeen, though the thought seems unlikely.

The Scots revel in their pawkiness, if that is the right word, and know as well as the Bard that a jest's prosperity lies in the ear of him who hears it, never in the tongue of him that makes it. Boswell did not cavil when Dr. Johnson exclaimed, "Prospect, Sir! The finest prospect a Scotchman ever sees is the road to England!" And the lad from Auchinlech rushed for his notebook when the Doctor snorted, "Oats are a form of food eaten by horses and Scotsmen."

At the beginning of the 19th century, a similar joke was going the rounds. "All you need to do to catch a Scotsman is put a bowl of porridge out overnight," said the wags. They may not have had Penang in mind, but by then the island was becoming a great porridge trap for the younger sons of Scotland's impoverished gentry, as Sjovald liked to remind me. Here were to be found the Gardynes, the Lindsays, the McAlisters, the Machills, the Sparrens, the Macrells, MacIntyres, the Carnegies, the Colquhouns, the Duffs, and many others including James Scott himself, partner in business with the late Francis Light. All of them (except the soldier MacAlister) were engaged in private enterprise of one sort or another, and soon they were joined by a young relative of Scott's from Lanark called David Brown, who became a junior partner in the firm of Light & Scott, now renamed Scott, Brown & Company.

Many of these Penang Highlanders as the English dubbed them, had been ruined by their forebears ill-starred attempt to restore the Stuart dynasty in 1745. Brown's own grandfather Robert Cunyngham fought in Scotland as a field officer with the Lamont and MacGregor Clans to which the Cunyngham belong, had been proscribed by the English victors, losing name and land, and his grandson David seems to have been equally belligerent. Before he had been in Penang 18 months he was already active on a committee to protest against the newly-appointed Superintendent Major Forbes Ross MacDonald; and once that much-pestered and over-wrought soldier fled to Calcutta with the story of his woes (where he almost immediately died under an avalanche of correspondence) the island sank back into its own version of peaceful existence.

Clopping down the streets in their smart little turnouts, dining in each others' houses, holding dances and receptions, entertaining passengers from passing East Indiamen and drinking rather a lot, they saw to it that life was not all work and no play. And the local Asian population began to understand, with amusement, that the sense of humour of these foreign devils was very similar to their own — a recognition that grew stronger over the years and became, as much as anything else, the link that held East and West together in shared affection.

About this time, an event occurred that caused an increase in Penang's territory. The Napoleonic War was still dragging on and Spain being on France's side, Britain was contemplating an attack on Manila, the capital of the Spanish Philippines. Early in April 1797 there appeared a 28-year-old Lieutenant-Colonel of the 3rd Foot Regiment named Arthur Wellesley — later to become the famous Duke of Wellington — who had been given command of the Manila Expedition.

The future Iron Duke arrived at Penang with a fleet of transports and while waiting for further orders from Calcutta (which never seemed to come) took up his residence in a fine pillared mansion along what is now known as Northam Road.

While the officers danced and flirted with all the pretty girls, even the Ranks solaced themselves — not by any means alone — in the dusky shadows of the bamboo grove between Light Street and China Street (which soon became known as Love Lane).

Colonel Wellesley passed his time drawing up a plan for the defence of Penang. He saw at once that the island must be sure of its own 'back door'. The previous year Scott and Brown, together with a committee of angry citizens, had made a number of sensible suggestions about this, which might have been followed had they not been so rude to the wretched Major MacDonald. Chiefly these concerned 'Defence against attack from the Mainland opposite' which was not surprising after the close shave a few years before. After studying their paper the Colonel decided to refer the question to his elder brother, Richard, who had just been selected by Pitt to be Governor-General in India. If Richard (now Baron Wellesley) agreed, it would be necessary to make approaches to the Sultan of Kedah for the grant of a strip of coastal land — say from the Sungei Muda down to the Sungei Krian — with enough hinterland to give it adequate protection. He urged that this should be done without delay.

In due course the expedition to Manila was called off, and having briefed his brother concerning the needs of Penang, the Colonel departed to join in the defence of Tipoo Sahib at Seringapatam (a stepping stone, perhaps, to his close-run victory at Waterloo) leaving the East India Company's administrative machine to negotiate with the Sultan of Kedah and devise a new treaty covering the new territory as well as Penang Island.

As a result Sir George Leith, Bart., endowed with the new title of Lieutenant-Governor of Penang, was able to proclaim formal possession of Britain's first territory on the mainland of the Malayan peninsula, which was named Province Wellesley. But this was merely the prelude to the island's emancipation from Cinderella to Princess.

Penang was now destined to act as a springboard for greater things; for the founding of Singapore, and for the subsequent opening of the peninsula to trade with the Malay States behind their hitherto locked doors — indeed of Malaya's progress from feudalism to a muddled 19th century type of Westernisation in little more than a single generation. Had it not been for Penang, there would have been no fulcrum for Britain's next thrust into Southeast Asia. And Britain would almost certainly never have gained possession of Singapore.

These were things that the bewildered baronet could hardly have foreseen as he took up his new appointment. So far as he was concerned, he had simply stuck his head into a beehive, and at the bottom of it were those cantankerous Scotsmen. Led by James Scott and David Brown, they were embroiling themselves in every description of legal action; and then scornfully disregarding the Lieutenant-Governor's decisions as being ultra vires in the absence of a properly constituted Judiciary for Penang. The miserable man was almost driven frantic. Finally he successfully begged Calcutta to send down a qualified judge, only to be further mortified when Mr. Justice Dickens repeatedly gave judgements to which Leith was totally unsympathetic. And when he openly opposed them (as he was sometimes rash enough to do) there was an appalling dust-up with the Scotsmen.

Worst of all, George Town caught fire in 1803. The centre of the town was completely gutted, and half a million dollars worth of damage was done. When Sir George Leith left for India at the end of his tour of duty, his only consolation was the reflection that the pepper plantations were coming on splendidly and that a vessel of 300 tons had just been built and launched by Penang's first shipyard.

This at least was justification for retaining Penang as a settlement. Ever since the time of Lord Cornwallis, Fort William had been trying to shrug off the place in favour of the Andaman Islands. But now that English oak was growing so scarce, the possession of a place where naval vessels could be built of Asia's magnificent teak had become a matter of over-riding importance, and the launching of this teak-built 300-tonner set the seal on the wisdom in choosing Penang.

From now on, thanks to ship-building and pepper, there was less talk about the Andamans. In fact the Company, after years of niggardly neglect, suddenly rushed to the other extreme.

Behind this change of mind lay a compelling reason; for by over-running Holland, Napoleon had caused the Dutch East Indies to become enemy territory. With such a menace slap in the middle of the vital trade route to China, it was necessary for Britain to set up a naval base immediately to guard the Straits of Malacca. And that meant a naval base at Penang.

In London, the Government ordered the Company's Court of Directors to get busy and sanction the necessary funds at once — funds that could only be considered if Penang were not a minor settlement but a full-scale Presidency like Bombay or Madras.

To take such an astonishing decision, the Directors were encouraged not only by the ship-building potential and the arrival of 3,000 tons of pepper from Penang (which went straight to their heads) but also by the enthusiastic dispatches from a remarkable newcomer called Robert Townsend Farquhar, who had taken up his post as the new Lieutenant-Governor of Penang on 1 January 1804.

Swept away by these considerations, the Court of Directors promptly sanctioned an orgy of spending — all because Penang was to be elevated to the dignity of a Presidency. Farquhar was to have his naval base south of George Town, partly on a small island called Pulau Jerejak (where a minute fishing village had been pompously renamed James Town by its owner, David Brown, in anticipation of the event). He also received approval to build an enormous brick aqueduct all the way down from the waterfall, four miles inshore, to the middle of George Town. But poor Farquhar was not allowed to enjoy the fruits of his endeavours. He was transferred to make way for a completely new Presidential government. And on 18 September 1805, the Hon. Philip Dundas (son of Viscount Melville, Chairman of the London Board of Control) arrived as the new Governor of the Presidency of Prince of Wales Island and Province Wellesley. With him landed a whole staff of writers, a Council of three members, a Chief Secretary, and a young Assistant Secretary named Thomas Stamford Raffles.

7. Tom Raffles Arrives

Let us take a look at this young man as he follows his wife down the gangway and steps into one of the *sampans* that are ferrying the governor of the new Presidency and his entourage ashore.

He walks with a slight stoop, giving the impression that he is not very tall; despite the heavy chest, his legs seem disproportionately long for the rest of his body. Tawny hair frames an open face whose somewhat leonine expression is marred by a slight cast in one eye. At 24, Thomas Raffles admits to being 'as meek as a maiden from want of self-confidence and natural shamefacedness' (as he wrote to a friend) but packed with energy and 'insatiable ambition'.

His upbringing had been far from easy. He was born in 1781 — the year that the British army surrendered at Yorktown and America became independent — aboard the West Indiaman *Ann* as she sailed from Jamaica in a convoy of 200 vessels. Most of these ships having carried slaves from Africa to the Caribbean, were returning to Liverpool loaded with rum and tobacco.

Though his father, Captain Benjamin Raffles, was engaged in this lucrative trade as Master (and possibly part-owner) of the *Ann* he died heavily in debt, leaving the boy to support his mother and sister. At the age of 14, Tom had to leave the Mansion House boarding school in Hammersmith and take a job as temporary clerk, or office boy, at the East India Company's headquarters in Leadenhall Street. His salary was £70 a year, and all we know of the ten years that he spent at East India House is that Charles Lamb, the essayist, and Charles Wilkins, the pioneer orientalist, were there, too; and that during those ten years young Raffles made his mark as a conscientious worker. In his free time, he taught himself French and studied literature and science, often staying up so late at night that his mother complained of his extravagance with candles.

It was the decision to turn Penang into a Presidency that gave Raffles his chance for promotion. The young clerk's merits had not gone unnoticed, and when the Hon. Philip Dundas was appointed Governor, he chose Raffles to accompany him as Assistant to the Chief Secretary. The appointment carried a salary of £1,500 a year, nearly 20 times what he had been previously earning, and within a week, Raffles got married. His wife was an Irish woman named Olivia Fancourt, the widow of an assistant surgeon in Madras. As he very reasonably remarked, "When I was about to quit all other ties and affections, it was natural that I should secure one bosom friend." Later, Lord Minto described Olivia as a 'great lady with dark eyes, accomplished and clever.' But the fact that she was ten years older than Raffles caused idle tongues to wag. It was whispered that the price of his job had been marriage to the discarded mistress of one of the directors.

There is no evidence to validate this unkind gossip, or that he ever took any notice of it. Clearly they were a devoted couple, despite the difference in their ages. Which was just as well, for the next five months' voyage out to Penang on a rolling East Indiaman was hardly a honeymoon cruise. No more than bare living space was provided aboard, and passengers had to make do with such essentials as they had brought themselves. Yet somehow Raffles managed to learn

Malay during the trip, which was more than his colleagues had any intention of doing.

If his journey out was enlivened by intellectual discoveries, his landfall was one of confirmations. Settling down to improve the Malay he had taught himself aboard ship, Raffles soon began to master the intricate local politics of this far-eastern region, and at the same time shouldered half the jobs that his Chief should have done. Olivia was fascinated by the way Mr. R as she called him, was always doing everybody else's work for them. She didn't mince her words, either, about the 'pompous and ignorant dullards' with whom they had to mingle. She considered Mr. Dickens, the Judge, to be blatantly dishonest and 'the most insufferable and conceited old jay you ever saw.' They had one great consolation. Their health was sound for they lived high on a hill above the sea some four miles west of George Town, and then in a newly-built seaside house called Runnymede where the constant breeze off the sea blew away the mosquitoes. They managed to survive whilst so many others died.

Luckily, while poking his nose into places which no one else bothered to inspect, Raffles came across a Scottish assistant surgeon, almost at the point of death in 'a kind of naval tavern where all around is ringing with vociferations of tarpaulins, the hoarse bawling of sea oaths and the rattling of the dice-box'. Raffles took him home to be nursed back to health by Olivia. For his part, John Caspar Leyden responded with torrents of marvellous talk, pouring out a wealth of knowledge, punctuated by acute comments and dry Scottish humour. They fell under his spell.

The strange romantic friendship arising between the huge gentle Scotsman and the newly-married couple may have been a tale of three intellectual people who found themselves living far from home in an uncongenial society. Their friendship had crucial results. For Leyden's researches into Eastern languages and habits, together with his enthusiasm for botany and zoology, acted as a catalyst on Raffles' mind. Leyden was a genius and a poet. From him Raffles gained the inspiration to begin his famous botanical and zoological collection; and eventually to found (and indeed become the first president of) the great London Zoo. It was Leyden, moreover, who first brought Raffles to the notice of Lord Minto, the Governor-General of India. But for Leyden, Raffles might never have achieved international fame as a scientific investigator, or won the necessary backing to become an empire-builder. The seeds that led to the founding of Singapore were sown by Leyden in Penang.

In this fertile friendship Olivia played a part because, had it not been for her, Leyden might never have gained their mutual affection. Indeed, after Leyden died of fever in the arms of his dear friend Raffles some years later, Olivia herself gently wilted away. Her body lies in the grave next to his at Tanah Abang in Java, with Leyden's own words, scribbled years before on board ship as he left for India, inscribed in marble on her tomb:

...But Chief, that in this Eastern Isle,
Girt by the green glistering wave,
Olivia's kind, endearing Smile
Seemed to recall me from the Grave

Meanwhile Raffles was making his mark in Penang. There was an enormous amount to be done; docks and an arsenal to be constructed; teak imported from Burma to build ships; municipal amenities extended; houses and shops erected. He took over the Court Registry, which was in an appalling state, and handled the correspondence not only with the authorities in India but with the local nobles on the mainland, which he was able to conduct in Malay. "Being of a cheerful lively disposition and very fond of society," remarked Captain Thomas Otto Travers, "It was surprising how he was able to entertain so hospitably and yet labour so much… not only in his official capacity, but in acquiring general knowledge of the history, government and local interests of the neighbouring states, and in this he was greatly aided in doing by conversing freely with the natives who were constantly visiting Penang at this period, in their own language."

According to Travers, Raffles carried the whole burden of the administrative machine. Although his colleagues thought him too big for his boots, and disliked the way he cultivated the friendship of the Malays, most were content to sit back and let him do the work.

Before long he was sent to Acheen in Sumatra to negotiate a trade agreement with the Sultan. This he handled so well — appreciating the Malay point of view and hammering out a policy that gave Penang's merchants reasonable rights without allowing them to ride roughshod over everyone else — that the Sultan of Acheen made him a Dato (approximately a Knight) and gave him a golden sword.

Shortly afterwards Calcutta decided that the town of Malacca, which had been in British hands since 1795, should be demolished to prevent it from competing with Penang once it was handed back to the Dutch when the Napoleonic War ended. Raffles was sent down to report on the progress of the demolition, which was to include the compulsory evacuation of the entire population and their forcible resettlement in Penang. Since the inhabitants had lived in Malacca for centuries, he realised that the whole scheme was an example of bureaucratic insanity.

Raffles' dispatch to the East India Company was one of the most compelling pieces of reporting ever to reach Fort William. It not only convinced the Governor-General of the cruel folly of the order, but resulted in Raffles being called in 1810 to Calcutta for consultation in 1810. There with Leyden's help, he became

Lord Minto's personal friend and protégé. His period as Assistant Secretary in Penang was over.

Minto now sent Raffles back to Malacca, this time as his personal agent. With the greatest secrecy he was to investigate the chances of a scheme which he himself had been thinking of, and which had been in Minto's mind for some time. This was to invade Java and capture Batavia. The capital of the Dutch East Indies, it was the headquarters of Holland's Island Empire of the Eastern Seas.

Malacca was the nucleus of a web of traditional trade-links and channels of communications between the Sultans of States throughout all Southeast Asia, including Java. It was the ideal spot in which to test and shape Minto's secret Java plans. Here Raffles was to sound out the opinions of ruling Chiefs in all the adjacent countries. Their goodwill and agreement were essential to any such enterprise, and Raffles was the only man who could be trusted to handle them tactfully.

This he did, and following his favourable report an expedition of some 90 ships left Malacca in June 1811 under the personal command of Lord Minto. They took six weeks to reach Java, passing close to the swampy island of Singapura on the way. By 4 August, the whole fleet lay off Batavia (now known as Jakarta). There was very little fighting, for the plan was to treat the Dutch as friends and allies who had merely suffered the misfortune of having their mother-country overrun by France. Indeed after a purely token resistance the Dutch in Batavia flung their French cockades away. It was one of the shortest campaigns on record.

In recognition of the role he had played in planning it, Raffles was appointed Lieutenant-Governor of Java. Minto was sure he would govern it in the interests of the Javanese until it was returned to Dutch hands. "Let us do all the good we can while we are here," were his parting words to Raffles as he left for Bengal.

Certainly during the four-and-a-half years that he ruled Java, Raffles did his best to replace the mercantile monopoly practiced by the Dutch with a more liberal free-trade system, which would allow British traders to compete with them. Personally he hoped that the British occupation would be permanent; though it was clear that when peace came, Britain would probably find it expedient to give back to Holland her overseas possessions.

Time was too short for Raffles to be able to do much in Java. His destiny lay elsewhere.

8. The Coup of The Century

Meanwhile life at Penang continued — and sadly all too often didn't.

Every now and then the Penang Highlanders dashed across the stage; a team of bearded businessmen with faces like Aberdeen terriers to protest against some legal injustice. Inevitably these forays ended in a great session of boozing and cursing the Governor; or flared into furious arguments as to whether MacAlister had not been improperly selling their own private supply of whisky (one shouting match ended with MacAlister chasing McHill down the street with a horsewhip.)

The apparatus of social life flourished, as the *Prince of Wales Island Gazette* recorded in 1807:

> *On Thursday, being Lord Mayor's Day, Mr. Robinson entertained a select party of friends at his mansion on the north beach. In the evening a most elegant fête was given by Messrs. Clubley and Phipps. It is impossible for us to convey any idea of the style and manner in which everything was concluded.*
>
> *The Honourable the Governor, together with the whole of the beauty and fashion of the island assembled at an early hour.*
>
> *The Ball commenced between eight and nine. Mr. Clubley had* the *honour of leading* Mrs. *Raffles down the first dance to the tune of 'Off she goes.'*

The supper rooms were thrown open at precisely twelve o'clock. The tables were covered with every delicacy that India can produce. The wines were of the most delicious quality; and that nothing might be wanting to render gratification perfect, several ladies and gentlemen entertained the company with songs, displaying on the one part the utmost delicacy of taste, and on the other true original comicality.

Dancing recommenced with increased life immediately after supper and continued until an early hour in the morning, when the party separated with every appearance of regret,

"That time should steal the night away
And all their pleasures too -
That they no longer there could stay,
And all their joys renew."

In addition to the musicians of the island, Captain Harris was so good as to allow his band to attend. They played several pieces in a very superior style. One of the performers danced a hornpipe à la tamborina, which bore strong marks of his being a perfect adept in the art, and called forth loud and reiterated bursts of applause from his fair beholders.

Which governor presided at this festivity it is difficult to say, so appalling was the death rate from malaria in those days. Both Philip Dundas and his wife lasted barely six months. The wife died and Dundas, who was put aboard a ship leaving for Madras, succumbed as it left the harbour. His tombstone in the Northern Road Cemetery records that he died in Penang.

Clearly the island was not the health resort that everyone had thought it would be. Sir David Bruce came out to replace Dundas, and lived just long enough to become a popular figure with all races before dying, too. There followed a Mr. Petrie and then a Mr. Seton from India, both of whom joined the long line of victims.

Yet even as malaria was carrying off Seton — only days after he had assumed office — the authorities at Fort William were studying the depressing trade figures and wondering whether the decision to turn Penang into a Presidency had been wise. For hardly had the huge expansion in the island got under way than the pepper boom which had inflated their hopes came to an end.

An elderly colonel named Bannerman was sent down with orders to retrench, and suddenly there was no money for anything. The roads clogged up with mud during monsoons; people became uncomfortable and grew bad-tempered. Yet curiously some of Penang's most historic buildings were erected during this period.

It was during Bannerman's tenure of office that a young engineer officer named Captain R. N. Smith built to his own design (in the intervals between painting pictures of Penang that have become famous) one of the most beautiful small churches in the whole of Southeast Asia, namely the Church of St. George the Martyr in Farquhar Street. Bannerman's daughter Janet was the first person to be married in it. Her husband was William Edward Phillips, an ex-army officer who arrived at Penang in 1800 as secretary to Sir George Leith, and had been acting as Governor when Bannerman took over.

Phillips, a man of taste, bought Francis Light's Suffolk estate from James Scott in 1805, but was unable to build on it due to lack of access. Finally an Indian laundry-woman (nicknamed the Queen of the Dhobies because she had a monopoly on the tubs) agreed to sell a portion of her dhobie-ghaut beside the bridge over the Pinang River near the present Methodist Boys' School, thereby enabling Phillips to erect a magnificent mansion on the foundations of Light's old garden house. He named it Suffolk House and when he lent his place to his father-in-law in 1817, it became the official Government House. This it remained after Bannerman died and Phillips became Governor in his turn.

General James Welsh, who married Francis Light's daughter Sarah, thought it one of the prettiest spots he had ever seen: 'In the midst of a fine extensive lawn, surrounded by majestic trees and a box hedge, with a clear brook meandering through the center, stands the noble and gracious house with a park and aviary in front and the hill gradually receding in the background, crowned with woods of the richest foliage. Italy itself could not produce a more verdant or lovely landscape.'

Even Lord Minto wrote to his wife in Scotland that 'Mr. Phillips is magnificently lodged; and his house which he built himself, is one of the handsomest I have seen in India. This mansion is not quite in proportion to the island, and looks like the great lady in the little parlour.'

While Suffolk House was his memorial, Phillips had greater call to be remembered with affection by Penang; for it was during his period as governor that a law was passed abolishing the age-old system of slavery throughout the territory which came under the island's jurisdiction. Other countries, including the United States, did not follow suit until about half a century later. But Penang took the lead.

One wonders what thoughts passed through Martinha Rozells's mind as she looked back on the wild love of her childhood — the adventures and struggles, the sorrows and the failures that had finally led to fame and success. The old 'First Lady' of Prince of Wales Island was still living in the house built by the sea down Martinha's Lane that Francis Light had built for her and their family. (Eight years after Light's death, James Scott had bought up all his urban land adjacent to Martinha's house in defiance of Light's Will, giving rise to the saying that 'Scott was true to Light unto death — but not a moment later.')

In 1799 Martinha had married a Mr. John Trimmer, and her brood of children by Francis Light were launched into the world.

Sarah, the eldest, married her general; they returned in 1817 and stayed at Suffolk House. Mary's husband was a well-known indigo planter in Bengal; at the age of 16, little Lukey became the bride of a doctor in Calcutta.

William, the eldest son, had a career as remarkable as his father's. After escaping with a school-fellow from revolutionary France at the age of 17, he returned to Penang to see his mother in 1805. Three years later, William joined the army and fought right through the Peninsula war, ending up as a Colonel; on his return to England he married the natural daughter of Charles, third Duke of Richmond. (The Lights seem to have established a hierarchy of well-connected illegitimacy.) The couple then spent some years cruising round the Mediterranean in their yacht, during which time William painted some reasonably good pictures, met up with Byron and Shelley in Pisa, and became commander of Mohamed Ali Pasha's navy in Egypt. Finally he sailed to the new colony of South Australia, and just 50 years after his father had hoisted the Union Jack at Penang, he achieved immortality in his turn by founding the city of Adelaide, now twined with Penang.

The younger son Rollo or Lanoon (pirate in Malay) Light as he was often known, having been born during the battle of Prai against Kedah in April 1791 — was the only one of Light's children to settle down in Penang, after marrying Caroline d'Urban in England. She was a relation of William's former commanding officer, Sir Benjamin d'Urban, who captured Natal in 1842 and gave his name to the city of Durban. Like Rollo himself, she may well have had Eastern blood on her mother's side, for it is sometimes said that he married a Javanese lady; at any rate these two are the ancestors of the few Lights who remain in Malaya and Singapore.

By now, of course, Raffles had become Penang's most notable figure though an absentee. Bannerman always referred to him grumpily as The Golden Sword — hadn't he made up to Minto so disgracefully, and with such phenomenal success?) Yet Raffles had his troubles, and some sorrows, too. World events and envious tongues were soon to rob him of his Lieutenant-Governorship of Java. Lord Minto died; John Leyden and his beloved Olivia both followed his patron to the grave.

In 1816 Raffles was recalled.

He took back to England 200 cases containing his collection of oriental carvings, textiles, plants, stuffed animals, folk art, and notes for a history of Java. Once this monumental work was published in 1817, Raffles found himself lionized. He was made a member of the Royal Society and introduced to the Prince Regent's daughter; before long Queen Charlotte, the wife of mad old George III, was asking to see the treasures that Raffles had brought back from the East. Diplomatically he had dedicated his *History of Java* to the Prince Regent, and one Thursday he was commanded to a levee at Carlton House. After congratulating him on his book and his administration in Java, the Regent gave him a knighthood.

Enjoying as he did the friendship of the Royal Family and the esteem of England's leading men, it is surprising that Raffles consented to be fobbed off with the minor post of Lieutenant-Governor of Bencoolen in Sumatra. With Princess Charlotte pulling the necessary strings, he could look forward to any position he wanted in England; it was even hinted that he could expect a peerage and the Governor-Generalship of India once she became Queen. What's more, that winter he had met and married his second wife, Sophia. Yet with every inducement to the contrary, he was determined to go. The outpost of Bencoolen was only a springboard, 'My Elba' he called it.

Before leaving London, Raffles submitted a paper to the East India Company stressing how vital it was for the China trade that Britain should establish her power convincingly in the Malay archipelago. Now that Malacca had been returned to Holland, both

Penang and Bencoolen were too remote to curtail Dutch activities. England needed another settlement at the mouth of the Straits to safeguard the passage from India to the Chinese seas. He pressed the Company to occupy Rhio or Singapore before the Dutch got there first.

The authorities in London held back; they were chiefly concerned with keeping the Dutch happy. But in India Lord Hastings was less inclined to be fooled by Dutchmen who, having had their Eastern possessions restored to them by virtue of British arms, were now playing havoc with British commerce. He saw clearly that the Chinese trade must be protected, and that Raffles was the man to do it. Sir Stamford was therefore summoned to Calcutta and instructed to found a settlement at Rhio or failing that, at Johore. He was told that the government of Penang would provide the necessary men and stores.

Raffles needed no prompting. From the frigate bound for Penang he wrote to his friend Marsden that his sights were set on Johore. 'You must not be surprised,' he told the historian of Sumatra, 'if my next letter to you is dated from the site of the ancient city of Singapura.'

At this point our history begins to resemble the scenario for a golden-age movie.

As the hero sails into Penang, he is greeted with the news that the baddies (the Dutch) have already occupied Rhio and are claiming rights over Johore. What's more the Governor Colonel Bannerman is furious with Raffles for poaching, as he sees it, on his preserve. He refuses to supply either troops or assistance, arguing that further instructions are necessary from Bengal now that the Dutch are in possession. The Golden Sword says Bannerman caustically, had better return to Bencoolen.

Raffles is of course quite unperturbed. There are social scenes at Suffolk House, with cocked hats and wraps of gold assembled for a

Ball. As the beauty and fashion decorously twirl, Sir Stamford sets about fooling the malicious colonel. Sipping a glass of claret, he agrees to remain in Penang until an answer from Lord Hastings is received. They both know that this will take months (but Raffles knows that he already has the okay for Johore in the bag). During dinner, he craftily persuades the mollified Bannerman to allow Farquhar (the Resident of Malacca who had been seconded as his assistant) to proceed with the frigate and some small ships to survey the small islands off Java. After more copious quaffing, the Governor agrees.

Now comes the cloak-and-dagger stuff. Raffles makes a great ploy of setting up household with his wife, Sophia, who is pregnant. A few days later, Bannerman and Raffles stand on the quayside waving goodbye as Farquhar's expedition sets off. But while the little fleet is waiting for the tide outside the harbour, Raffles sends out a boat with a message saying that he will be following the next day in a merchant ship, the *Indiana*. That night she is secretly got ready, and at dawn he sets sail, leaving a note to be delivered to Bannerman (once his ship is safely over the horizon) explaining that he had gone to keep an eye on Farquhar's activities.

Off Rhio, Raffles catches up with the others. Farquhar thinks it's a good spot for a settlement. Raffles disagrees, and gives orders to set sail for the island of Singapura. There the ships anchor off the mouth of the river. A few *sampans* and *koleks* float idly in the calm waters; some Malay children are playing among the coconut trees that fringe a fine sandy beach. It is 4 pm on Thursday 28 January 1819.

As soon as they have anchored, a group of local inhabitants come aboard. Raffles asks to see their Chief, a prince of the House of Johore who is styled the Temenggong. Next morning Raffles and Farquhar call on this dignitary at his rush hut under the palms. Raffles explains that he wishes to start a settlement and will pay a good rent. The Temenggong says he would be delighted, but the decision rested with the Sultan of Johore.

Raffles knows very well that the Sultan is in the pay of the Dutch, so no chance there. But, clever chap, he also knows that the succession to the throne of Johore is in dispute, for on the death of the old Sultan the younger son had seized the crown. What then does Raffles do? Why, of course, he sends for the elder brother, who is living in exile, to restore him as legitimate heir.

The 'rightful heir' arrives in a small boat, is installed as Sultan, and promptly signs a treaty granting Britain all the facilities that Raffles wants. (The offer of 5,000 dollars along with a gift of opium and arms probably encourages him to take this wise decision.)

As the Union Jack is hoisted, Sir Stamford declares that hence and forevermore, Singapore is to be a free port and, leaving Farquhar as Resident (under his authority) sails off into the setting sun.

The coup of the century has taken him just a week.

9. The Great Tin Boom

This latest incartade of Sir Raffles as the Dutch ambassador at the Court of St. James fumingly described it (meaning everything from insult to folly in diplomatic parlance) was of deep significance to Southeast Asia. On Raffles' orders, Singapore was initially controlled from far-off Bencoolen, whose Lieutenant-Governor had instigated the whole affair. It shifted the focus of British interest from Penang to Singapore — which was not only better situated as a commercial port but also a more strategic naval base. This also led to a sensible if simplistic division of interests, whereby 'everything on the starboard hand going down the Malacca Strait on the way to China will belong to the Dutch; and everything on the port hand to the British.' By the Burney Treaty of 1825, Britain got Singapore in exchange for Bencoolen.

After the land swap with Holland, the East India Company administered Province Wellesley, Malacca and Singapore from Penang. However, in 1835 the capital of the Straits Settlements was moved to Singapore.

Increasingly the strength of the Straits Settlements began to shake Southeast Asia from its age-old lethargy. New ideas came flooding in from the West to send awakening ripples north to Thailand, east as far as the Sula Sea; Penang and its daughter Singapore were to share the responsibility of bringing the winds of change to the Malay peninsula, along with the concept of a multiracial society.

For although Penang's population was largely composed of Chinese of one denomination or another, there were also a considerable number of Malays and Indians.

By religion, the Malays were without exception Muslims, who sprang from the three small kampongs which Light had found on his arrival and the any others who came across, mainly from Kedah. There were also thousands of Malays from Perlis and the Langkawi Islands who came pouring down to the safety of British-owned Province Wellesley. They were fleeing from the invading Siamese (it was that old question of tribute with Kedah again) and so seriously did they upset the tapioca and sugar-growing economy by camping and trampling everywhere, that the Governor of Penang offered them permanent title to all lands they chose to open and cultivate for themselves along the north coast and as far round as the south-west tip of the island itself, including the large and until then jungle-covered western plain of Balik Pulau. These successive groups of refugees were the first genuine Malay settlers on Penang Island since Dato Andor had worked his clearing at Dato Keramat in 1707. The remains of the earliest Muslim Mosque on the island, which was built by these newcomers in 1821, are still visible, interlaced by the roots of a Javanese banyan tree, at the village of Telok Bahang.

But there was also a significant group of Indian Muslims, likewise of the Sunni branch of the Muslim faith, who were descended from generations of Chulia merchants. And these were now joined by the transfer of Bencoolen's prisoners — often courageous men of good family and high tradition who had been involved in some feud or other in India or had fallen foul of harsh laws and brutal circumstances — along with other Muslim Indians who originated from officers and soldiers of the Indian regiments stationed on the island.

At the Sultan of Perak's request, moreover, the Penang government took over Perak's coastal lands, known as the Dindings and before long this area, which hitherto had been a wilderness inhabited only by pirates was converted into valuable agricultural land. (It was handed back to Perak in 1933).

Indeed by the middle of the 19th century, the shape of the Malay peninsula was accurately known; by 1840 the entire Malacca Strait had been sounded, with some supporting land survey; and charts were printed by the British Admiralty in 1842. But the dense jungles behind the coastal plains still served as a barrier against the advance of civilisation.

Certainly trade with Kedah had been open to foreign businessmen since Light took possession of Penang. And further south, Penang's merchants were also accustomed to working up river as far as the Perak state capital of Kuala Kangsar and even to Ulu Langat, the capital of Selangor. From the borders of well-trodden old Malacca (where a large kingdom known as Jehole was thought to stretch north through the jungle as far as the Siamese state of Terengganu) an intrepid character called Mr. Gray penetrated the swamps and mountains of Pahang down to the South China Sea, only to die of his exertions.

Of course, Johore in the far south of the peninsula was familiar to all, being synonymous with tigers and elephants and wild tribes of primitive jungle folk (in western minds, at least). But apart from such sporadic contacts — and hearsay from Arab and Chinese traders who had been in and out of the peninsula from time out of mind — comparatively little was still known about the genuine mainland Malays.

These sensitive and withdrawn people were known to be artistic and temperamental; kindly but easily roused folk who were largely uninterested in trade. They made beautiful boats and houses and produced laminated-steel weapons from their own forges; they were expert weavers on handlooms and designers of intricate fabrics in cotton and silk; they were exquisite jewellers and carvers of wooden fretwork. Their age-old stage and shadow plays, harking back to Indo-Aryan folk-tales, and their evocative *pantuns* (or rhyming quatrains) and fables re-telling their long history in fairytale romances, showed them to be an imaginative people with an immense tribal memory. Being of the Sunni sect, they were firmly traditional but not fanatical Muslims, reading from the *Qu'ran* in Arabic. They lived as they always had done; working their lands in feudal manner, going to mosque on Fridays, seldom moving far away from their kampongs and occasionally buying a few clocks, music boxes or other such exotic toys. Beyond that, this ancient folk had little use for western civilization.

Arab traders had for centuries intermarried with the leading Malay families, and this landed aristocracy controlled the Malay peasantry under a domestic discipline that it would be a mistake to describe as serfdom. The countrymen fished, hunted and tended to fruit orchards whilst their womenfolk bent their backs to the labour of padi-planting. A few Hokkien Chinese, settled for hundreds of years here and there about the peninsula, kept the shops, bought the harvests, and found markets for the produce. The way of life was a balanced symbiosis between Malays and Chinese, and there seemed no reason why matters should drastically change.

True, for centuries there had been talk about the fabled land of Reman with a mountain, so the story ran, composed entirely of purest tin. But in 1848 Tungku Sulong, the hereditary chief of two areas in Perak just south of Penang known as Larut and Matang, learnt that a rich deposit of tin lay right on his doorstep. The Hokkien Chinese from Penang, who had made the discovery, lost no time in securing agreements with Sulong and other chiefs to exploit these riches and a country-wide scramble for tin began. Deposits were searched for and found from north to south. Prices rose; and as contracts were given and land changed hands the Malays began to find themselves more and more in the hands of the astute Chinese financiers. Since labour for the mines was in urgent demand, people left their *kampongs* and the padi-fields became deserted. Money poured in and the old way of life came abruptly to an end as the country became the world's largest miner of tin.

Although this first great boom in tin disrupted the ancient patterns of Malay life, few people had any qualms. In the short term, they all gained, and the Hokkien Chinese, who gained most, were nothing if not a traditional part of the rural economy (the Big Five — the Tan, Yeoh, Lim, Cheah and Khoo families — were already well-established as magnates and powerbrokers by this time. See *Appendix I*) They had helped Malay landlords over many bad seasons in the past; now they sparked off a new explosion of prosperity. So everyone was more or less happy.

And whilst this was happening on the mainland, Penang benefited. Fine houses, built by Malays as well as Chinese, began to mushroom up throughout the town; Love Lane, Armenian Street, Stewart Lane and Muntri Street became gracious areas, and Church Street proudly displayed its unique Hokkien meeting hall known as the Ghee Hin Kongsi; Pandora's box had been opened.

Yet in northern China a plot was hatching which was destined to trigger off a new incursion of an even more virile race of Chinese into Malaya and render the Hokkien presence a mere trojan horse for their arrival.

Since 1644 a usurping dynasty from Manchuria known as the Ching had sat upon the Dragon Throne. Though countless uprisings against them had failed, the flame of revolt aimed at restoring the old Ming dynasty had been kept alive by a secret society known as the Hung League or *Tien-ti Huey* (also called the Triad or Heaven-Earth Society) from their strongholds in Canton, Szechuan and the outer borders of China. The toughest members of this cult had always been a tribe called the Hakka or Khek people who were sometimes thought to have originated in the outer steppes. These Hakkas tended to remain aloof wherever they were to be found. Indeed their very name Khek meant guest or stranger; or even gypsy.

In 1851 the greatest of all rebellions to restore the Ming broke out, and went on for 15 years. No war in Europe had been so deadly. Finally the Ch'ng government called on the west for help and in the end Colonel Charles Gordon (Chinese Gordon as he was always called until he became known as Gordon of Khartoum) helped to quell the Taiping Rebellion in 1865.

As a result, some 45,000 Hakka field-officers and their families were exiled from China. It took eight years to ship them all away. Every year from 1865 on, these exiles went down in their thousands by junk during the northeast monsoon to the Philippines, Borneo, the Dutch East Indies and above all to Singapore — from whence they rapidly spread all over Malaya and especially Penang.

The land administrations in Malaya were unable to cope with this flood of foreigners, and indeed were opposed to accepting them. On the mainland, therefore, the Hakkas concentrated on carving out holdings in the jungle. They went up distant rivers, into the mountains or along mangrove-infested coastlines, in every inaccessible corner where they could lead their lives undisturbed.

But in Penang they found themselves amidst an antagonistic community of Hokkien merchants, who hated these blustering foreigners with their unknown tongue, and had no interest in their cause. And so many of the Hakkas settled higher up the slopes of Penang Hill, where their descendents are still landed farmers. But others set themselves up downtown in violent competition with the Hokkiens.

Moreover these Hakkas soon began to infiltrate the tin industry as well; opening mines, bribing village headmen, and carving out Chicago-like spheres of influence for themselves ('pay so much every month or you'll have a bad accident') in the process of which they sometimes set man against man, chief against chief, and State against State.

For ten years the placid atmosphere of Penang was disrupted by periodic rioting. Secret warfare between the rival factions of *See-kuans* composed largely of Hokkiens, and the *Ngo-kuans* who were mostly Hakkas, flared into open street-fighting during which barricades were thrown up and all business came to a stand-still. Houses were burnt down, batteries of heavy cannon were fired in the main streets of George Town; bloodshed was almost a daily occurrence and every man took his life in his own hands. Over on the mainland, the Malay rulers became involved, one against another; and gradually the whole peninsula from the Siamese border to the Straits of Johore grew into a bloodbath.

Their dissatisfaction stemmed from the local administration's inefficiency and Calcutta's absolute refusal to support any expansion of business on the mainland. Calcutta took the view that if merchants chose to trade with the Malay States it was on their own responsibility and they could expect no help whatsoever from Government if they got into trouble. There were moments, especially between 1869 and 1871, when the harassed officials in George Town must have felt there was little difference between what was going on at their own doorstep and the sacking and burning that was happening at the same time in Paris under the Commune.

By making their voices heard at last, the business community had succeeded in shaking the Straits Settlement out of the lethargic grasp of the Indian administration and placed directly under the Crown. After years of Parliamentary lobbying in London led by a former resident of Singapore, Dr. James Crawfurd, together with a number of influential citizens, this transfer was accomplished in 1867. Penang's Transfer Road which neatly demarcates the boundary of the town at that time, commemorates the island's emancipation into a Crown Colony.

Penang was growing in commercial importance — not only through the steady increase in trade with the mainland, but also because of the change in the Settlements' status. But as it happened, the improvements expected from the new dispensation were slow in coming, for ironically the last Governor sent from India was the most popular the Straits Settlement had ever had, whereas the first 'Queen's Governor' from London was perhaps the worst and most detested. If Colonel Sir Orfeur Cavanaugh was a fine red-faced, peg-legged old soldier with a taste for port and an eye for the girls, Colonel Sir Harry John Ord turned out to be a dyspeptic snob whose interest centred chiefly on receiving handsome presents from the Malay rulers.

And on the mainland the political situation was growing steadily worse.

For one thing, a feud had broken out over the succession to the throne of Perak. And open warfare was raging between two rival Princes in Selangor. Battles between Malays and Chinese were going on in the area down south known as Sungai Ujong. Moreover piracy at sea and highway robbery on land had become everyday occurrences, while the struggle for tin in Perak's rich areas of Larut and Matang was driving the Hakkas and Hokkiens to senseless butchery. Some British firms had lent money to the *See-kuan*; others to the *Ngo-kuan*, and were consequently taking sides. The feud spread to the business mart of Singapore as it already had done in Penang. Under the pretext of enterprise commercial rivals were busily distributing to one side or another such 'somewhat unconventional items of mining equipment as rifles and brass cannon.'

At last Colonel Anson of Penang, who was acting as Governor while Ord was away on leave, used his initiative and intervened.

Off the Selangor coast, a Chinese junk flying the Union Jack had been captured and sacked by pirates. Their stronghold was the Fort at Kuala Selangor, which had also become the headquarters of Raja Mahdi, one of the two princes quarrelling over the Selangor throne.

Anson ordered *HSM Rinaldo* and *Pluto* to capture this Fort, which after a sharp action, they did. Whereupon tin shares took an upward leap and disorder declined. A respectful note crept into the correspondence from ruling houses on both sides of the Malacca Strait to the British Government.

Incidentally the guns removed from the Fort at Kuala Selangor were brought to Penang in *HMS Pluto* and being of no interest to the garrison were dumped into the sea at the naval anchorage. Among them was a most beautiful bronze cannon cast in 1603 by the famous Jan Bergerus of Amsterdam. Discovered and brought ashore later, it now stands on the ramparts of Fort Cornwallis bearing the quaint appellation of *Meriam Timbul* (Floating Cannon) and lovesick women make offerings to it on grounds of phallic association.

Great however was the rage of the avenging Ord when he returned from leave. 'A rash act' he fumed. 'Against orders...highly dangerous...wasting tax-payers' money to assist the private profit of the business community.' All must be undone, he decreed, the Fort must be returned, and negotiations for trade with the mainland States dropped immediately.

He failed to take into account the infuriated reaction of this same 'business community' who, stung beyond endurance by his contempt for their interests, resigned en-bloc from the Legislative Council and made use of the new 'submarine cable' to send a complaint to the Secretary of State for the Colonies.

As a result, Ord was recalled. Jubilation still rings down the ages in the press accounts at the departure of 'this unhappy Governor; and his shipload of loot.'

"We offered you our love," were the newspapers' parting words to him, "You chose our hate."

10. Expanding Horizons

By contrast, Colonel Sir Andrew Clarke of the Royal Engineers was just the man that the business communities of Penang and Singapore had been praying for.

Breezy, confident and bright, the new Governor heralded an awakening interest in Malaya's intricately tangled problems. London, it seemed, had finally understood that the policy of non-intervention in the internal affairs of the peninsula was meaningless, however well-intentioned.

After all, British presence in the Straits Settlements had already caused old allegiances to change and balances of power to alter. Clearly intervention had started with the arrival of Francis Light. Kedah's increasingly bellicose attitude towards Ligor and its overlord Siam; the disputed succession in Perak; the now rich and powerful Chief of Larut's demand for status as an independent country (which had actually been approved by Ord); the bloodshed and piracy leading to the affair at Kuala Selangor — all these developments had stemmed from the landing at Penang 90 years earlier.

And so, armed with an entirely new set of instructions that were the best he could wring out of the Colonial Office before accepting the appointment (basically they were to 'ascertain and report' on how to restore peace and protect trade) the new Governor set to work. He applied these injunctions with what Northcote Parkinson described as 'a majestic liberality of intervention.'

Realizing that it was no use just talking to Rulers when the heart of the problem was caused by Chinese millionaires pulling the strings behind the whole shadow-play, Sir Andrew Clarke sailed up to Pangkor in Pluto and there he called a memorable meeting with not only the Malay and British dignitaries, but also the *See-kuan* and *Ngo-kuan* leaders.

The outcome of this gathering was a document signed on 20 January 1874 and known as the Engagement of Pangkor. By this, the Chinese agreed to submit all disputes to a British committee for arbitration, whose findings they would obey. They also agreed that a British official would reside in Perak to advise the Sultan and his Council on matters other than the Muslim religion and the customary laws of the land.

"All right, all right," commented Sir Andrew, "I know. I was told to ascertain and report, so I took action and reported afterwards. If the British Government doesn't like it they can kick me out — thank God I don't depend on a pittance from the Colonial Office." And there are still Malaysians who have cause to be grateful to him for being so constructively disobedient.

Now all that had to be done was obtain Queen Victoria's assent to the agreement, and Britain would be committed to sorting out the chaos and opening up the peninsula for commercial development. Nevertheless, in the words of the Duke of Wellington on another occasion, it was a 'damn close-run thing.'

For Queen Victoria refused point-blank to give her assent. In the wake of the Indian Mutiny she was opposed to Britain taking on fresh responsibilities or being involved in the control of any other lands. Had it not been for Prime Minister Disraeli's persuasive wheedling —

'But Ma'am, oppressed people, fever-ridden swamps, blood-smitten wilderness, work of humanity, Ma'am' it is doubtful whether Britain would ever have set foot in the Malay states.

As it was, the Queen eventually gave in, as she always seemed to do under Disraeli's magic spell. But she only gave her approval to the Engagement on the understanding that those who went out to administer Malaya would, in her own words: "Bring on the peoples of those countries to the stage where they can govern themselves."

It was perhaps unfortunate that Sir Andrew Clarke left the Straits not long after this, for his place was taken by Sir William Jervois, who seemed anxious to outshine his predecessor by making an even more aggressive impact upon Perak.

Sir Andrew had appointed his own Colonial Secretary, James Birch, as Adviser to the Perak Sultan, and this unfortunate official misunderstood the situation there. Convinced that rivalries among the Malay chiefs would prevent them from effectively opposing his advice to the Sultan, Birch overlooked the fact that on one point they were not in the least divided — and that was their opposition to himself. Not content with writing over-optimistic reports to Singapore, he pressed on with innovations ranging from the suppression of 'slavery' to a new system of taxation that would benefit Government but be ruinous to the riverside Chiefs who from time immemorial had taxed all traffic on the river.

On Jervois' arrival, Birch was commanded to make sure that the Sultan carried out these changes, even though they ran counter to traditional practice and involved tampering with the customary laws of the land. Moreover when the Sultan and Council of Elders dug in their toes with unexpected stubbornness, Jervois merely abrogated the terms of the Pangkor Engagement and appointed Birch as Queen's Commissioner in Perak, with powers to carry out the measures whether the Sultan agreed or not. In the words of *The Straits Times*, Jervois had taken a stick and given the hornet's nest a good poke.

But the stick was too short. Even as the first notices of his new position were being posted up on public buildings in Perak, a band of Malay chiefs dashed into Birch's bathroom on the boat where he was taking his morning shower. After spearing him to death, they flung his body into the river (having first hacked off his head which floated downstream separately.) And so began a further stage in Britain's involvement in the native states, this time with troops and guns. The ensuing war cost much good Malay and English blood but did more, as Frank Swettenham later commented cynically, 'to bring law and order to the Malay peninsula in 20 months than could have been achieved by 20 years of peaceful persuasion.'

Well, maybe so, but there as also a pressing need to safeguard the export of tin, As a result, hasty arrangements were made with the contending parties and both the States of Selangor and the Negri Sembilan (the nine counties) also came under British administration around this time. These developments had the practical effect of opening the States to trade in peaceful conditions, and of bringing health, education, order and prosperity to much of the countryside. It can certainly be argued that they contributed towards the eventual emergence of today's independent Malaysia.

Incidentally, descendants of the Sikhs from the Indian Punjab, who were recruited by Captain Tristram Speedy for a chief of Larut, are now to be found in all the learned professions, in the Police — and as merchants, money-lenders, watchmen, railway employees and cattle-keepers everywhere in Malaya.

Penang benefited greatly from these events. Having lost its Presidential status and then its position as capital of the Straits Settlements, so that let alone the failure of its low-country clove harvests and the loss if its place as main entrepot to the up-and-coming Singapore, business had been in the doldrums for nearly forty years. But now matters began to improve. Despite all the uproar and violence it had created, the discovery of tin on the mainland gave the Colony a much-needed shot in the arm.

This new prosperity made it possible to open many more clove and nutmeg orchards in the highlands of the island, and to cultivate large areas in Province Wellesley with sugar, tapioca and coconuts as well as planting Liberian coffee. But above all the port began to boom again once merchants and planters could penetrate the mainland.

For the next few decades — until roads and railways were built throughout the peninsula in the early 20th century — all the trade with north Malaya and southern Siam was carried by ship from Penang. Glorious mansions, such as those in Logan Road, Perak Road and indeed some of the older ones still to be seen along Northam and Kelawei roads, indicate the affluence of the Chinese merchants from 1875 to the end of the century. As peace and progress grew on the mainland, the up-country towns came into being. Coffee plantations opened in Perak and Selangor; business people built offices and homes in the capital towns of both these States. The Malay peninsula was in need of everything from brandy and bottled beer to road-building and agricultural machinery — all of which, together with export shipments of coffee, sugar, oil, tin, tapioca and spices, passed through the port of Penang.

The lighthouses of Muka Head, Fort Cornwallis and Pilau, as well as George Town's fine Town Hall on the Esplanade and the great government building in Beach Street, were all built during this period. Now, too, the city began to develop the glory of its shaded avenues and flowering trees. From 1861 onwards the Arboreal section of the new Municipal Engineering Department planted carefully selected saplings along all the country lanes which spread out from the centre, with the result that the suburbs remained beauty-spots. Along the city's thoroughfares great angsana trees (the trees of 'golden rain' angsana) began to drench the air with the heady perfume, and shower down a mist of yellow petals when the first rains came after the dry winter weather.

Out in the countryside the padi fields were lined with slender grey-barked Pinang or areca nuts palms after which the island is named; their delicate foliage and red clusters of nuts stood charmingly out against the green brilliance of the young rice and the dark backcloth of jungle. Coconut palms bent their sleek heads against the monsoon, while majestic royal palms stood a attention like giant soldiers on parade outside public buildings.

Cassias, copper pods, tulip trees, flame-of-the-forest, red flowered coral trees, *lilac lagastrumia* and red bohinia blossomed in the January sunshine; blue cascades of jakaranda petals whirled across the poinsettias and banks of bougainvillea.

Even then, as a change from the dark-green beauty of the Javanese banyan-trees — chattering with fruit-hunting birds and cool shady nooks — were to be seen that strange African curiosity, the *baobab* tree, of which one still bulges like a squatting elephant at the corner of Peel Avenue and MacAlister Road.

Yet even as the island was sunning itself so placidly (and profitably) in the noontide of British imperialism, a new plant was brought in that would transform the whole country. Queen Victoria's Diamond Jubilee year saw not only the establishment of Perak, Selangor, Negri Sembilan and Pahang into an entity called the Federated Malay States (FMS) with its capital in a new town known as Kuala Lumpur, but also the advent of the rubber tree.

Twenty years earlier, while exploring the upper tributaries of the Amazon, a young painter named Alexander Wickham had helped himself to sackfuls of seeds from the Brazilian India-rubber tree — the *Havea Brasiliensis*. This small consignment was eventually planted in Kew Gardens, and in due course, a few seedlings were dispatched to Peradeniya Gardens in Ceylon.

At that time Malayan planters in Perak and Selangor were busy clearing their newly-acquired lands and putting in coffee. Several of these men had come from Ceylon, and as coffee plants need shelter from the wind and the sun when young, they decided to interplant rows of these little havea saplings to act as windbreaks and give shade. It occurred to them that when mature, their juice might even have some commercial value.

But from 1894 onwards, the bottom dropped right out of the coffee market. Coffee from Brazil (which had been robbed of her rubber seeds) was now swamping world markets. Prices slumped from $48 to $18 a hundredweight, and the finest Liberian coffee beans were being used to feed steam-engines. Faced with this situation, Malayan planters began to take a fresh look at their sturdy young rubber trees. Tests showed good returns from the juice or latex, and before the end of the century several plantations were made entirely over to rubber

Thus, coincidental with the emergence of bicycles and the early motorcars, came the first great boom in Malayan rubber.

By 1904, the year of the first rubber auctions in London, plantations were being hacked out of prime jungle. Bullock cart tracks followed by winding metalled roads were beginning to thrust their way through the western swamps and mountains of the peninsula.

Rising to fever peak between 1910 and 1924 this tremendous development altered the face of the country and brought vast riches to the ports of Penang and Singapore, enriching the government's coffers. At the same time it enlarged — and submerged — the existing population.

Peninsula Malays, who considered themselves *Bumiputra* or princes of the land (and the denomination was quite well-known even then) preferred, as descendents of land-owning families or possibly even landowners themselves, to stick to rice farming. So Dravidian Hindus from South India were recruited in hordes as labour for the plantations. One hundred thousand Tamils were ferried each year from Madras to Penang by the British India Steamship Company alone, accompanied by Indian merchants and petty traders, and this influx continued unabated for ten years.

Moreover whilst this mass migration was pouring in, including tens of thousands of Ceylonese Tamils for work on the new railway system, a separate invasion was occurring.

Six to eight thousand enterprising Chinese, their eyes casting around for possibilities of gain, came sailing down from Hong Kong and China's coastal ports aboard the British-owned Shan Line every month. And this, too, went on for ten years

To Malays it must have seemed that no country but theirs was ever subjected to such a cataract of humanity. This ancient and traditional people, whose way of life had remained unchanged for a thousand years, was suddenly smothered under a tidal wave of foreign activity, and rushed through a millennium of evolution in the course of one life time. Perhaps it had to happen. The purely material benefits to Malaya were vast. But whether these material advantages were worth the almost total obliteration of the Malaya way of life remains a moot question.

Seen in this light, the Malaysian government's determination to re-assert the rights of the Malays in their own county now that a united nation has emerged at last, is readily understandable. It also explains the uneasy jostlings and unfriendly gestures that are still at times perceptible between the various peoples of this land. Indeed nothing but sympathy, patience, and unceasing goodwill for those of all races in Malaysia who have undergone so much, can safely lead through into the future.

But one fact should be stressed. Unlike the horrors of King Leopold's rubber empire in the Belgian Congo (where some 800,000 sq miles (1,287,475.20 sq km) of territory were held in subjection by an army of mercenaries who wiped out most of the native population), or of Julio Cesar Arana's domination of the wild rubber forests of the Amazon (worked until 1910 by 30,000 chained slaves, hundreds of whom were shot as they stood chained in rows) the introduction of rubber into Malaya was accompanied by no bloodshed, brutality or grave injustice.

Rubber, did, however, change the whole infrastructure of the mainland, as well as its geopolitical situation (to use two present day catch-phrases). Notably it drew in the north-eastern States, whose suzerainty to Buddhist Siam was, if anything, a historical accident.

During the early days of the 20th century a railway had been completed from Singapore to Bangkok. It ran up Malaya's west coast and linked several branch lines from the Malacca Straits ports. Subsequently an east coast railway was planned to fork off in northern Johore and, after passing through Pahang, run through the middle of Siamese Trengganu and Kelantan.

But it so happened that an enterprising Scotsman named Duff had recently taken out various concessions over large tracts of land in Kelantan from the Siamese government, through which the proposed railway line was intended to run. Legal proceedings were begun by the Straits authorities, but the problems of acquiring so many different Siamese land titles were so complicated that it was finally decided to send an experienced official from the Malayan Civil Service to sort out the tangle. The upshot was a recommendation that, provided suitable arrangements could be made with Siam ad the two Sultans, both Trengganu and Kelantan should be placed under a form of British protection stemming directly from the Governor of the Straits Settlements. Johore, it was pointed out, had entered into a similar transaction with Britain in 1882.

Meanwhile in the northeast of Malaya, Kedah and Perlis were becoming more and more involved in business with Penang. Their connection with the Settlement had been close for over a century, and a British financial adviser as well as various European engineers had long been employed by Siam in Kedah.

To add a note of comedy, Captain Berkeley, the District Officer of Upper Perak, was rumoured to be sedulously moving his boundary-stones further and further north every year, so that the British-protected Federated Malay State of Perak began to thrust forward into the heart of jungly southern Siam like a dagger. When the British High Commissioner, having vainly attempted to call Berkeley down to headquarters by messages that never seemed to get through, finally went down himself to investigate, he was put off by a laconic statement sent by runner from Berkeley that there was 'No bridge at the 42nd mile'. So he returned to Kuala Lumpur unaware that there had never been a bridge at the 42nd mile.

All these factors culminated in a proposal to Siam that the Straits Settlements Government should be permitted to open negotiations with the Sultans of the four States of Trengganu, Kelantan, Perlis and Kedah to accept some loose form of overall British protection. In return for which Britain would bear certain costs of the existing west coast railway as well as the projected east coast one.

The fact that Siam had never made any profit out of these countries and that being Muslim states they would welcome the chance to join their brother Malay states under a more or less common administration, rendered negotiations easier. As a result, Trengganu came under British protection in 1909, Kelantan in 1910, to be followed in 1911 by Kedah and Perlis. They were known as the Unfederated Malay States (UMS) and, like Johore, took their general policy direct from Singapore.

Thus the future State of mainland Malaysia was defined; and though Longfellow did not have it in mind, his words were appropriate:

Sail on, O Union, strong and great!
Humanity with all its fears
With all the hopes of future years
Is hanging breathless on they fate!

11. Rubber And Opium

Apart from handling so much of the mainland's valuable produce, Penang had a secret weapon of its own. For over a century, a separate golden thread had run through its history, bringing riches to many of the island's leading Chinese families.

In India, princes and potentates had traditionally derived their wealth by auctioning out the various public utilities in their kingdom. And from its formation in 1600, the East India Company had followed this practice, adopting the old Elizabethan term of 'farming' to grant licences for meat selling, liquor shops, gambling, brothel-keeping, and notably the production and sale of opium to the public.

On the arrival of the Presidential government in 1805, this system was introduced to Penang. Chinese merchants would bid for one or the other of the monopolies and by the middle of the 19th century the auction fees for the farming of opium alone amounted to between 45% and 66% of the Colony's total revenue.

Despite comment from various quarters that the Colony 'lived on its vices', no good reason was seen to amend this procedure when the Crown took over in 1867 — perhaps because the Straits government saw no practical means of abandoning it.

Indeed, although an organised lobby against the opium traffic had been gathering momentum in England since 1874, it was not until the end of the century that public-spirited young Chinese intellectuals in Malaya began to quote the Earl of Shaftesbury's Parliamentary Resolution of 1843 condemning the whole opium trade, and formed themselves under Dr. Lim Boon Keng of Singapore into an Anti-Opium Society.

From that moment on, in spite of opposition from Chinese vested interests, matters gradually crept forward until 1907, when Britain appointed a Malayan Commission of Enquiry to study the question of the opium traffic in the Straits Settlement and throughout the Malay peninsula.

On the commission's recommendation, the system of annually auctioning out the opium trade to the highest bidder was finally abolished; and the Straits Settlement's government itself took over the business of manufacturing and retailing a well-refined and comparatively innocuous form of opium to certified drug addicts only, that is, addicts who were re-certified by a qualified government doctor each month. Moreover a new arm of government service was recruited to combat smuggling and unauthorized vending or smoking of opium anywhere in the country. By such measures, and the diminution of licenses issued to authorised smokers due to normal annual mortality, the opium problem diminished and was practically solved by the time the Japanese war broke out in 1941.

Meanwhile the opium farmers of Penang, in the days when their trade was still universally regarded as perfectly respectable (and indeed honourable), lived in grand style and built many of the delightful houses that are still among the island's scenic glories.

Understandably, a feeling of envy, not untinged by malice, grew up between the mainland and the glittering cities of Singapore, Malacca and Penang. A sense of being different, almost a feeling of alienation, developed between the inhabitants of rough and tumble Malaya and the elegant lordlings of the cosmopolitan Straits Settlements. After generations of British rule, the Chinese in particular had begun to regard Penang as being almost a county of England — they referred to themselves as the Queen's Chinese.

This cosy link with Britain was never felt so strongly in either the Federated or the Unfederated Malay States, who were simply Protectorates being brought on, in Queen Victoria's words 'to the stage where they could govern themselves'. But during the 1914–1918 War and indeed for a period in the Twenties nearly all Malaya prospered so greatly that neither Malays nor Chinese or anyone else was preoccupied by the psychological difference between the Colony and the Native States. Most people were doing far too well to question the good fortune they had inherited from Britain.

Tin and rubber were successful; imports flowed from Penang and Singapore to every part of the peninsula. Good order and just laws prevailed; public health was improving fast; and education (free for Malays) was available not only from government schools but also from Catholic and Anglo-Chinese Methodist establishments that were springing up all over the country.

In Penang, the Saint Xavier's Institution had taken over in the 1860s from Father Garnault and Condé's small village school in Farquhar Street, and was already famous. A great seminary for Catholic priests in Pulau Tikus had grown out of Father Rechtenwald's original small school; and the Penang Free School, founded by the Reverend Mr. Hutchings in 1816, had already become one of the leading colleges of Malaya. The Sultan Idris College at Kuala Kangsar had just been opened to cater for the sons of Malay rulers and chiefs.

Every capital town throughout the country now possessed magnificent buildings for its State government, along with grandiose railway stations, Royal palaces, government hospitals, law courts, police stations, schools, clubs, playing fields, mosques, cinemas and churches.

King Edward VII Medical faculty of Singapore University was already training first-class doctors for private practice and government service. A survey department staffed largely by New Zealanders mapped every mile of the country; the mines department controlled tin and gold. Huge drainage and irrigation works were going forward in the mainland's various Malay rice-bowls. Agriculture, education, fisheries, forestry, geology, meteorology, customs and excise, veterinary and animal-husbandry departments, staffed by highly qualified professionals were the training grounds for young Malays, many of whom were then sent on scholarships to English universities.

Over the entire range of government, as Advisers in the UMS and as Residents in the FMS, as well as at the central secretariats and at the head of every department other than the Judiciary and the police, presided the highly-skilled Malayan Civil Service. Its officials were answerable to the Governor on the one hand, and to the people (through the Rulers and Headmen or Penghulus) on the other.

These MCS officers, selected by the Colonial Office in London, took up their work in Malaya as a permanent vocation, and were not subject to transfer outside Malaya. Never more than 300 in all, they spent their entire working lives in the service of the country, which they virtually created; and the three generations of officers which made up the short but not undistinguished history of the MCS are now looked on as having been the Pioneers, the Consolidators and the Polishers. With the gratifying feeling, as Gilbert would have said, that their duty had been done.

If this minute coterie administered a multiracial landscape, nowhere did they encounter a wider blend of humanity than in Penang. Here nationals from all over Europe mingled with Southeast Asians from the Celebes to Acheen; and these far-flung peoples worked, lived and played not only with Dravidian and Indo-Aryan races who stemmed from Ceylon to the Himalayas, but also with Chinese whose genealogies stretched into every corner of China from Hainan to Mongolia. For Penang was a melting pot in which the process of involution — not necessarily through cross-breeding, but through prolonged living side by side — merged in a discernible Penang mentality; an ambience which, though hard to describe, had rendered the European less western and the Asian less oriental both in features and ways of thought.

Of course (and how could it not be so) there was much intermarriage too. But whereas in India people of mixed descent referred to themselves as Anglo-Indians or Dutch-this or that as the case may be, in Penang they employed the proud and evocative term Eurasians.

Such families are to be found all over Malaysia, but especially in Penang. Descendants of Martinha Rozell's brothers remain elegantly English-Portuguese as do the Lights, who are now mostly in Singapore. The great-great-grandchildren of countless early settlers are still in evidence, some showing more strongly than others the influence of generations of Indian or Chinese blood. The Gregorys take after their Siamese great-grandmother and their French great-grandfather, a marine engineer called Louis Carrier. The Smiths and de Souzas are intermarried; the Lows are related to the French Boudvilles, and the Boudvilles to the Cornish Balhatchets, as well as to leading Chinese families in the area. The Jeremiahs, whose ancestor came to Penang with Francis Light in *Eliza* in 1786, have long been connected with Siamese and Indian merchants on one side of their family, and with the Wymmis family on the other — as are indeed the Lows and Carriers. The Scotts, Browns and Samuels intermarried over and over again to produce — with the introduction of blood from Portugal, Indonesia, Thailand and China — a typically Penang family identity in which the rugged

Scottish and Welsh blood has been warmed by the intellect and gentle intuition of Asia.

And this is to mention only the British connection. When it is realised that the other races of immigrants, including large numbers of Dutch families from Indonesia, and excluding the Muslim community, have been similarly intermingling their blood on the island for two hundred years, the distinctive free-and-easy personality of Penang becomes more readily understandable. In that old tag of Cowper's: 'variety's the spice of life, which gives it all its flavour.'

What's more the physical aspect of Penang was constantly being improved. In 1904 the beautiful Supreme Court in Farquhar Street was begun, and in the following year the first waterworks was completed at the back of Waterfall Gardens. Electricity spread throughout the town, and by 1906 the electric tramway was running, though somewhat shakily and noisily.

Asphalt roads were being built; and notably a series of village footpaths and pony-tracks that led more or less consecutively round the island were being connected to form a well-laid carriage road.

This was a great step forward. A metalled road had gone out as far as Tanjung Tokong for years; from that village it had been necessary to use a muddy track even to reach Tanjung Bungah. Along this footpath was a new hotel called the Spring-Tide, soon a favourite haunt for holiday makers, and just beyond that came the Swimming Club — an exclusively European affair, for no one but the crazy 'Round Eyes' went swimming in those days. A palm-trunk and wire fencing out to sea kept it safe from crocodiles (which though gone now, were at that time prevalent). To reach the northern beaches and the little fishing village of Batu Ferringhi, it was best to go by boat.

Two points of interest arise out of the construction of the road around the island. First, the large number of *keramat* (Muslim shrines) that are still to be found all along the road indicate that the Indian labourers who built it were involved in the secret combine of Shiah Muslim, Kali (or thug) Hinduism, and the Chinese Hung League, whose esoteric roots exist until today. Second, a Hakka community was discovered on the south-western tip of the island. The Hakkas had apparently been living there in complete obscurity since they first arrived in abut 1868. These farming and fishing folk (who were also great smugglers) had no desire to mix with any people but themselves; and it was only when news filtered through that they had their own Court of Law which had recently carried out executions, that the government reluctantly stepped in and built a footpath between Telok Kumbar and their own village of Gertak Sanggul.

After the circular road was completed in 1918, attention was focused on the heights. Twenty years previously, a private company had attempted to lay a cable railway to the top of Penang Hill, but the design was so faulty that it failed. Having come up from Singapore to declare it open, the Governor waited for hours while the device refused to budge, before returning home disappointed, with his undelivered speech in his pocket.

At the end of the 1914-18 War, plans based on an entirely different system were drawn up and A. R. Johnston of the FMS Railways was put in charge of them. After spending two years in Berne studying Swiss cable car systems, he began the work of construction. By 1922, the Penang Hill railway — an engineering feat unique in Asia — was completed and became one of the island's outstanding attractions.

If anything, Malaya almost enjoyed the war. Europeans of fighting age went off to get themselves killed in Flanders, or survive with the feeling of 'having done their bit'. But in spite of a few alarms, the entire peninsula only saw two instances of actual combat.

The first of these occurred in Penang.

At dawn on Wednesday 28 October 1914, the German raider *Emden*, commanded by Captain Karl von Muller, swept into Penang harbour audaciously flying the White Ensign. With a fourth funnel hastily erected of burlap and dunnage to simulate *HMS Yarmouth*, which was expected some time that morning, *Emden* swung round in the naval anchorage and placed herself practically alongside the Russian cruiser *Zemschug*. Whereupon, hoisting the German colours, *Emden* let fly a series of broadsides into the Russian ship, which capsized and sank within a matter of minutes. Then, having sunk the French destroyer *Mousquet* as it arrived from patrol, the *Emden* made off at high speed over the horizon.

Mousquet's bower-anchor in the Penang Museum — along with a wreck buoy some cable-lengths north of the Esplanade (where the fishing is excellent) and various French and Russian graves in the Western Road cemetery — are the only remaining evidence of this incident.

To explain the second event (which in some ways arose from the first) it should be mentioned that Germany and her Muslim ally Turkey were hoping to make trouble in the Straits Settlements by setting the Shiah Muslims against the infidel British. A plot was hatched; a well-known India-Muslim merchant named Kassim Mansour was implicated and condemned to death; after his execution in Singapore some undercurrents of ill-feeling began to stir among Muslims serving in the Indian units stationed there.

It should also be said that at the outbreak of war, by a typically English piece of good-natured folly, all German residents and visitors in Singapore had been told to regard themselves as interned in their own palatial Teutonia Club (now the Goodwood Park Hotel). Their servants were free to go anywhere; the Germans could continue to operate their own bank accounts. Indeed their English friends, who found it difficult to regard them as enemies, used to visit and sent them presents of flowers and fruits.

The action now moves into the southern waters of the Indian Ocean.

Shortly after his successful raid on Penang, Captain von Muller captured a heavily-laden collier called the *Exford.* Having put a German prize crew aboard this vessel under the command of his navigating officer, Jules Lauterbach, he ordered her to lie off Cocos-Keeling Island ready to refuel the *Emden* when required.

However, while her crew was ashore on Cocos Island dismantling the submarine-cable station, *Emden* was unexpectedly pounced upon by *HMS Sydney* and battered to bits. Also intercepted, the *Exford* was taken to Singapore, where Lauterbach and his crew of German sailors were interned in the Teutonia Club.

In this atmosphere of civilian unreality (one of the first questions put to the German prisoners was whether they would join in a tennis party) Lauterbach and his shipmates had other ideas. They were soon able to make contact with the 5th Indian Light Infantry Regiment from Bengal that had been stationed in Singapore for years. Shiah Muslims to a man, they were now furious at being ordered to leave for Hong Kong. Lauterbach also contacted the Malay States Guides (all Sikhs from the Punjab) who, having refused to go fight in East Africa, were suspected of having been involved in the Turkish Plot and were virtually in detention.

Plans were made, orders were given, money changed hands (lots of money, for the interned German businessmen had access to large funds) and an uprising was organised to take place on Monday 15 February, which was the Chinese New Year.

From the German point of view, everything went splendidly according to plan. British army officers were killed by their own men; the Telegraph station was sabotaged and its staff butchered. What with houses burning, guns firing, everyone running in all directions and the Indian troops in open riot, the Singapore Rebellion was well on its way by six o'clock on that grey, rainy evening. Indeed it was quelled only after a week of heavy fighting.

Meanwhile Lauterbach and his friends were also well under way. Extricated by wire-cutters from the Teutonia Club, they drove in a commandeered car to Singapore's north coast and captured the ferry to Johore. There they broke into the Sultan's palace and obtained signed orders from the Sultan himself at pistol-point, instructing his officers to give them every assistance.

Then, after hijacking another car, they made for the east coast of Johore, where they boarded dug-out canoes and rowed down the Mawai River to the small port of Sedili. Here they seized a sailing craft — a mere cockleshell, but the best they could find. In this frail vessel they eventually reached the Celebes; from whence, after an immense voyage for so small a tub, they arrived in T'singtao, the former German Naval headquarters in northern China.

Thus in the end, they made their way home to Germany. All of them, that is, but Lauterbach. He was given command of the new raider *Moewe* and continued to wreak havoc out East until the end of the war.

12. Boom And Bust

Though the First World War had come as a surprise, it brought increased prosperity to Malaya. Rubber and tin boomed more than ever, and German freighters could no longer make the inroads into the Colony's carrying trade that had been worrying British steamship lines for decades. German businesses were closed down, and German plantations sold for a song. Their place was taken by Britain's new allies, the Japanese, who bought rubber estates and sold bicycles and sewing machines, while competing with America in the purchase of Malayan products.

The wartime boom in tin and rubber tailed away in 1922. Prices were middling, and the end of the Twenties marked the point at which Malaya's luck ran out.

The crash on Wall Street caused a disastrous drop in demand. Rubber and tin prices plummeted, and much of Southeast Asia's trade in mining and agriculture ground to a halt.

Now began the heartbreaking process of repatriating thousands of workless South Indian labourers, who streamed through Penang in weekly shiploads home. Hundreds of British planters and miners left as well, hoping to find work elsewhere. And now there was the sad sight of weed-grown paths in once lovely gardens, of dust-laded billiard rooms in bankrupt clubs, of abandoned bungalows and broken shutters creaking in the evening breeze.

The slump of the early Thirties did eventually give way to a slow recovery, visible by 1935, and Penang once again began to prosper in the short wintry sunshine of late afternoon, as it were, before the terrible night set in. Improvements were made to the port; roads were lengthened and widened, and some handsome new buildings were erected.

Nevertheless there was a pervading feeling of unease. Close at hand the Japanese, who had replaced Germany as rivals to Britain in shipping and the supply of goods, virtually swarmed through the countryside, managing their ex-German rubber plantations, and infiltrating into every corner of the peninsula as brothel-keepers, photographers and jungle-haunting taxidermists. On the other side of the world, Hitler and Mussolini strode across Europe stirring up explosions of nationalism. Where could all this end, but in global conflict? And which side would Japan take?

When war finally broke out in Europe, Roosevelt declared the USA to be the Arsenal of Democracy in 1940. There were two significant results for Malaya. On the one hand rubber and tin boomed as never before, being essential resources of war. On the other, Japan automatically became a potential enemy of the Allies. For Japan could only produce a fraction of the oil that she needed, and America was threatening to impose a total sanction unless Japan cancelled her treaties with Germany.

Many eyes east of Suez turned to watch the reaction of Japan. Japan's Prime Minister Konoye, who favoured the Allies, tried to steer a middle course. As a result he was rebuffed by Roosevelt and resigned — to be replaced by the militant warlord, Tojo. Worse still, when France and Holland fell that same year, their Southeast Asian colonies with their oil, tin and rubber, became vulnerable to a Japanese invasion. After that, only a miracle could avert war in the East. Time was running out.

Since half of China's huge territory had been occupied by Japan, it was clear that the largely Chinese-populated Straits Settlement firmly supported the Allied cause. But the Malays viewed the developments with mounting disquiet. They feared that something much worse was about to happen.

The global slump of the Thirties had shaken their confidence in Western wisdom, and they were beginning to feel that they had made a mistake in allowing themselves to become so closely involved in Western affairs, even if only as suppliers of important raw materials. Britain had led them by the hand into a den of thieves; a struggle that had nothing to do with them was going to break out between two foreign giants who would kill their people and destroy their land. The Malays suddenly saw what it meant to be dragged into modern civilization. They had enjoyed its advantages; now they were going to have to pay for them. It was not a pleasant prospect.

The great Naval Base was in the course of construction at Singapore. But only when the situation began to worsen in Europe did the British High Command take a look at Penang, and start work on various defence arrangements in 1938. These included a heavy artillery battery at the north of the island and another at the southeast, to guard the two entrances. A spotting post was located at the hill behind Batu Ferringhi, and a light defence post at Tanjong Tokong. A chain of concrete pill-boxes was erected across the flat land between George Town and Bayan Lepas Airport.

Clearly these measures were inadequate. Later on, perhaps by 1943 Penang might have been able to put up a stiff resistance to seaborne invasion if the island had sufficient air cover and fighting forces. But the time was not given; neither were troops nor aircraft. More urgent needs in Europe and the Middle East left Penang undefended.

On 8 December 1941, almost at the very hour that Pearl Harbour was bombed, the Japanese invasion of Malaya began. General

Yamashita's troops landed simultaneously at the Thai ports of Songkhla and Patani, and at Kota Bahru on Malaya's northeast coast. Having sunk both *HMS Prince of Wales* and *Repulse* — Britain's only major fighting ships in Southeast Asia — off Kuantan three days later, the Japanese continued their invasion. Slicing down the mainland like a knife through butter, they pierced the thin defence lines at Jitra and Gurun in Kedah, and cut off Penang without bothering to take it. Within three weeks the peninsula was theirs.

The invasion came as a shock to the civil population of Malaya. Feverishly hoping for a miracle that never happened, the government remained tight-lipped and reticent. Even when the Japanese fleet had occupied Camranh Bay in French Indo-China just across the Gulf of Siam from Malaya (conveniently granted to them by the Vichy government) the Malayan radio continued to be fatuously cheerful. By 6 December everyone at Naval headquarters knew that a vast Japanese fleet with 43 transports was heading towards Malaya. But the impression conveyed to the public was that they were making for Bangkok on naval exercises.

Thus the news of the landings and the loss of the two great battleships seemed incredible; a chimaera. It was not until the first bombs fell on Penang, leaving 600 people wounded and 150 corpses in the streets that panic swept the town. As looting and firing broke out, the inhabitants realised, with bewildered terror, that they were in the midst of a war.

Then five days after the first bombing a shameful thing happened. The British fled. Acting on secret orders from the Governor of the Straits Settlements, Sir Shenton Thomas, nearly every Britisher in Penang and Province Wellesley was compulsorily evacuated by ship to the 'impregnable fortress' of Singapore. Under strict instructions to tell no one of their impending departure, they were to desert their friends just as the ship went down.

Fortunately for the Europeans' good name, not all of them stole away like thieves in the night. To members of the various religious Missions and Orders — priests and brothers, nuns in convents — the thought of evacuation never occurred for a moment. Some British troops under Major Andrews of the 1/8 Punjab Regiment, who had escaped from Kedah in small boats, refused to follow in the footsteps of the evacuees. A chartered accountant named Thomas and a lawyer called Balfour-Ross who were staying at Batu Ferringhi never heard of any order to evacuate Penang. And certain government officials who knew the penalties for disobedience and realised that they would be ruined for life if they failed to obey the order, nevertheless refused to abandon the people they served. Among these were the Controller of Posts, E. A. Staines, and the Chief Medical officer, Dr. Evans, who were far too busy attending to their duties to listen to any nonsense about 'running away'. But the rest obeyed orders. They left on the evening of 16 December 1941.

In consequence the Police force, deprived of its commanders, became completely disorganised. Panic set in. There was looting and smashing, burning and killing.

It fell to the local leaders to assume command. The editor of *The Straits Echo* issued hand-printed notices calling for public meeting. On the evening of 17 December some 500 of Penang's leading citizens gathered together and formed a body known as the Penang Service Committee. This consisted of three members from each of the four communities — Chinese, Malay, Indian and Eurasian. The editor himself, Mr. Manikasothy Saravanamuttu, was elected Chairman.

During the three days intervening between the departure of the British and the arrival of the first two companies of Japanese soldiers in the evening of 19 December, this committee reorganised the Municipal services, enrolled the Chinese and Eurasian Volunteer Companies into an effective police force with orders to shoot looters on sight (which they did); cleared the streets of corpses; repaired the wireless station; issued a daily news bulletin; lowered the Union Jack, and sent half-hourly signals calling on the Japanese to halt their repeated bombing of the town.

When the Japanese forces arrived, Mr. Saravanamuttu had no alternative but to hand over command to them. He did so with courage and deference, but it did not prevent him from being maltreated and thrown into prison almost immediately after the war — ironically on nearly the same date as Parliament was making arrangements for his trial as a traitor and collaborator.

So began Penang's nightmare — a story of tyranny, fear, torture, oppression and brutal executions — that was to last for a total of 1,354 days. Even so, it probably suffered fewer horrors than any other large towns in Malaya, due to the fact that Penang became a naval base and an Axis submarine headquarters. True to their naval traditions, the Japanese and German officers' conduct, in sharp contrast to that of their military counterparts, was usually polite and civilised.

In March 1942, the infamous *Kempei Tai*, an organization similar to the German Gestapo, made its appearance in Penang. The *Kempei Tai*'s chief targets were the Chinese (on the grounds that they were Communists or Kuo-Mintang supporters); the Eurasians (for being pro-British); and all the teachers of English in Penang's many schools, though they were now without work and thoroughly discontented, on the supposition that they were imbued by their profession with English leanings.

In an initial display of frightfulness, the *Kempei Tai* organised mass beheadings of men, women and children; other victims were starved, mutilated, and subjected to inhuman floggings or pumped full of water until their stomachs burst. Many people vomited with fear at the screams that echoed from their lairs at Batu Ubin, Maxwell Street and Navy House.

In the last-named building (James Scott's old town house which for nearly a century had belonged to the Convent of the Holy Infant

Jesus) foreign sailors from torpedoed ships were herded into cells, tortured and atrociously done to death. The names scribbled on walls and behind doors, with a pencil stroke and the pathetic word 'rub' jotted against each one, bore mute evidence of this ghastliness for some years after the war.

Over Penang spread the terrifying shadow of the Japanese Police Commander, Tadashi Suzuki, a nephew of Count Suzuki, who was then Grand Chamberlain of the Imperial Court at Tokyo. Known as the Head-chopper, this monster with long hair and bristling moustaches held public executions on the Esplanade at Butterworth at which he delighted in chopping off as many heads as he could with a samurai sword given to him by the Emperor, before boasting of his prowess when raging drunk at night.

Under this pall of fear, life had to go on, and the Japanese made some efforts to bring normal existence back to the town. They succeeded to the extent of creating a travesty of urban economy, in which the hoarding of supplies was punishable by death, corruption was rampant, and every man was encouraged to inform against his neighbour. Bathtub distilleries of local *arrack* were licensed in common with the farming out of brothels and gambling dens; macabre public entertainments were given, bands played, and monthly race-meetings were organised at the Penang Turf Club. Some schools were allowed to re-open to teach Japanese.

The town was becoming important as an Axis submarine base. It held many German sailors and technicians with whom certain shops managed to do black market business when chances came their way. The Japanese constructed two primitive radar stations — one on the highest peak of the hill and the other to the southwest behind Gertak Sanggol — and set up a mountain battery together with a spotting post behind what is now the Penang University. The German Navy erected a dumpy, utilitarian blockhouse between Fort Cornwallis and Light Street to serve as a torpedo store.

Apart from the absence of cars, Penang almost looked normal. While Francis Light's statue was tossed on to a rubbish heap, the statue of Queen Victoria at the Cricket Club survived. Having been tactfully encased by the Chinese in a circular tube of plywood with eyeholes in it for 'Her' to look out of (the statue was regarded as a living embodiment of her spirit and thus needed both air and light), the monument was not closely inspected by the occupying forces. They would march by and salute the Japanese flag perched on top whilst 'She' regarded them serenely from inside.

If the Queen's Chinese needed jokes such as these to keep them going, a further ripple of laughter was caused by Lieutenant Gould of the Gurkhas in the Penang prison.

Having refused to obey an order by the Japanese to announce on the radio how well the prisoners were being treated, he was beaten unconscious. Realising on coming round that there was no point in continuing to refuse, he obediently made the required announcements, adding at the end of each statement, 'Tell that to the Marines!' The Japanese commander, delighted that he had recommended them to the navy in this fashion, patted him on the back and gave him a good dinner.

Stories are current that several British civilians lay hidden in Penang throughout the entire Japanese Occupation, and if this was so it is an indication of the courage and friendship of those who protected them. There is certainly one recorded instance of Allied soldiers remaining at liberty. Four British Other Ranks hid out in the jungle-covered hill top behind Telok Bahang, where they were given food and other necessities by a neighbouring Chinese farmer and his son, called Peter and Paul Lim. One or more of the soldiers are said to have died but the others survived and returned safely to England. Peter Lim, who would certainly have been killed along with all his family if the Japanese had been aware of what he was doing, received a well-deserved Commendation from the High Commissioner of Malaya for his bravery.

Finally in mid-1945, the first Allied bombings which demolished the Japanese Naval Headquarters in the old St. Xavier's Institute building, heralded the end of Penang's long bondage. All through July, hundreds of B29s streamed south to bomb Singapore, and on 6 August 1945, secret radio sets picked up the news that the atom bomb had been dropped on Hiroshima. A week later, it became known that Japan had surrendered.

Between 11 August and 3 December, when Admiral Walker landed in Penang from *HMS Nelson*, the Japanese behaved with exemplary discipline, appearing genuinely anguished at what they had done while in a condition of frenzy under the stress of war. During the interim period the former Penang Services Committee was reconstituted with Mr. Saravanamuttu as Chairman to head the civil administration. Thus, though thin and bedraggled, the representatives of all four communities stepped forward — Mr. Khoo Sian Ewe for the Chinese, Dr. (later Sir) Mohamed Ariff for the Malays; Mr. N. Ragavan for the South Indians; and Captain Willweber for the Eurasians, with Mr. Khoh Sin Hock (a direct descendant of the famous Khoh Lee Wan) as Secretary, were once again in charge of their city.

And, with almost the entire population lining the streets, waving flags and yelling a chorus of jubilation, the survivors of Penang's ordeal gave Admiral Walker and his liberators a truly royal welcome.

13. The Malayan Union

Nevertheless, the seeds of change had been sown. Indeed the whole peninsula was soon to experience a convulsion that would alter its condition more than the Japanese occupation had ever done.

Admittedly the invasion had not affected everyone in quite the same way. It was largely the Chinese townspeople who had suffered most, especially in Singapore and the mainland cities. Towards the Malays themselves the Japanese had been careful to adopt a conciliatory, almost ingratiatory attitude.

Consequently the rural administration had continued in Malay hands, and many who were living in isolated *kampung* never saw a Japanese. Orders from their new masters came through the Malay District Officers, *Penghulu* and village headmen as they always had, and since these kampung folk needed little from the outside world their sufferings were minimal.

Many of the forest people, the *Sakai*, those gentle diffident men of the jungle streams and mountains — the *Semelai*, *Jakun*, *Senoi*, *Semang* and *Temiar* — had never heard of the Japanese. Their only contact with world events were occasional news of Chinese camps on the lower slopes of the mountains, or of strange *orang puteh* (that is, Britishers) encountered on forest paths carrying guns. Other than that, life in the virgin jungle continued undisturbed. But now even this was to change.

Roughly speaking, the population of Malaya was now half Malay and half immigrant — of which the great majority were Chinese. By founding first Penang and then Singapore, the British had altered the ethnic structure of the peninsula. The Hokkien tin rush and the arrival of the Hakka hordes during the previous century had destroyed the ancient balance between Malays and Chinese. Western commerce had caused the Malay aristocracy to be steadily superseded by a British governmental hierarchy; rubber had drowned the country in a deluge of imported labour. But whereas the First World War had shackled Malaya firmly to the West and brought amazing prosperity to the country, World War II had caused it to be ruined by a foreign invasion.

All these factors combined to form an explosive situation.

If the Malays had been compelled to make the best arrangements that they could with the invaders, the Chinese had continued to be mentally or physically at war with the Japanese throughout the occupation. There was no Malayan nationality in those days; the Chinese in Malaya were either British subjects — such as those in the Straits Settlements — or subjects of China. Since both China and Britain were at war with Japan, so were they.

However just as there had been two major and quite distinct Chinese race-groups in Malaya — the long-resident Hokkien and the Hakka newcomers — likewise they had been split into two opposing political ideologies since the emergence of Communism in China.

By the time the Japanese landed in Malaya this internal dissension, inflamed by the Japanese invasion of China, had reached a boiling point. If the majority of the Chinese in Malaya were in favour of General Chiang Kai-shek and his forces (known as the Kuomintang) there were also many, especially among the Hakkas, who were wholehearted supporters of the new Communist doctrines.

When war broke out in Malaya a considerable number of both Kuomintang and local Communist Chinese supporters went into the jungle, ostensibly to fight a guerrilla-type war against the Japanese with arms and ammunition supplied to them by the Allied Forces. However, there seems remarkably little evidence of any combat on their part against the Japanese (possibly through fear of reprisals) but plenty to indicate that when not fighting bitterly against each other in the jungle (which often happened) the Kuomintang supporters remained virtually inert, whereas the Communists — who were imbued solely with the objective of taking over the whole of Malaya after the war — contented themselves with endless 'indoctrination' courses, along with occasional hit-and-run raids against civilian supporters of the Japanese regime and government administrators, who were naturally Malays.

The complexities of this situation were beyond the grasp of a war-weary Britain. Ashamed at the debacle in Malaya, the Colonial Office forgot that the peninsula had never been made ready against an enemy attack — that untrained troops had been rushed in at the last moment, and been denied any effective air cover. It forgot that the Malay States were not British colonies, but Protectorates with their own separate loyalties, which were merely being brought on to self-government. There were different yet interlocking regulations between the Straits Settlements, the Federated Malay States and the Unfederated Malay States. Viewed from London, the fault seemed to lie in the dispersal of command. All this needed to be straightened out; the administrative structure of the country must be simplified.

To implement these ideas, a few remnants of the Malayan Civil Service who happened to be in Britain were formed into a body known as the Malayan Planning Unit, an idea that had come from Edward Gent, holder of the Malayan desk at the Colonial Office, and Ralph Hone of the War Office. The result of their deliberations was a new policy known as the Malayan Union. By this, Singapore was to be a separate country under continuing British control, whereas all the States in Malaya were to be united together. Penang and Malacca were to be included within this Union, whose capital was to be Kuala Lumpur; their people would become Malayans whether they were British subjects or not, irrespective of their wishes. Indeed almost every inhabitant of Malaya would automatically become a Malayan and be accorded a vote. The object of this plan was that the Malay States should gain their independence, but remain commercially dependent on Singapore, which Britain would retain.

Lord Curzon's nephew, Sir Harold MacMichael, was hurriedly sent out as a special envoy to obtain the Rulers' agreement. But while reflecting no discredit on the emissary himself, this move merely served to underline the ignorance of Malay psychology. When the details were announced, there was a sense of shock throughout the peninsula, and uproar broke out. The Malay reaction was one of incredulous dismay at the abrogation, as it was considered, of Britain's many treaties with the Rulers.

The Rulers themselves were in a state of polite bewilderment after a long period of restricted residence and still faithful to their old belief that Britain was acting in the best interest of their people and themselves. They were given little time for consultation and pressed to sign the agreement urgently; however one of them is rumoured to have lost no time in cabling to the Colonial Office that he had signed under duress.

In contrast, the reaction from all sections of the Chinese population was one of jubilation. By gaining full nationality, the Chinese could go on building better lives for themselves in the land of their adoption.

Finally, almost lost in the turmoil were the plaintive objections of Penang, which was about to be so unexpectedly ejected from the British family to which it had devotedly belonged for over a century and a half.

Immediately after the war the government of the country was temporarily handed over to a mixed body of civilians and military officers known as the British Military Administration (BMA). Faced with a daunting job of reconstruction, the BMA did its best (even if the activities of a discreditable minority caused it to be labelled the Black Market Association). But the mounting anger of the Malays and the growth of militant Communism among some of the Chinese clans were quite beyond its powers to control. By the time the Civil Government returned in March 1946, the situation was already serious.

A Communist dock strike among Chinese workers in Singapore and Penang created havoc with industry and delayed rehabilitation. Being largely Malay, neither the Government's administrative staff nor the Army and Police, could be relied upon in their mood of angry pride at the insults from the Chinese and the way, as they saw it, that their country had been betrayed to these boastful aliens. Ill-feeling between the Malays and Chinese, together with a growing irritation at the British for having caused the problem, was becoming explosive. Racial clashes broke out in Johore, in Perak, and indeed throughout the peninsula.

It was at this point that Dato' Onn bin Jaffar, the son of a notable former Prime Minister of Johore, appeared on the scene. Being a District Officer in the Johore Civil Service, he realised that an armed uprising among the Malays was imminent.

A Captain Mohamed Salleh of Simpang Kiri in Johore had raised a troop called the *Parang Panjang* (the Long Swords) and already butchered all the Chinese inhabitants — mostly old men, women and children — at a village named Bakri near Muar. Along the Perak River and elsewhere around the country, other Malay irregulars were embarking on a campaign of wholesale massacre — such as that which took place with at Lambor Kanan in Perak.

These men were determined to revenge themselves upon the Chinese who had killed so many of their friends during the Japanese

Occupation. They intended to fight against the British idea of giving people they regarded as hostile foreigners equal rights with themselves in their own land.

Dato' Onn took leave from his post of duty at Batu Pahat and toured the whole country from end to end. By forceful argument with the Malay leaders and angry Malay crowds, and by reiterating his conviction that the British were a 'fair-minded and decent people who would put matters right when they understood what a terrible mistake they had made' he eventually persuaded them to lay down their arms.

Forming a party known as the United Malays National Organization (UMNO) he directed the Malays' fury along constitutional channels instead of resorting to bloodshed. He made it clear that his object was to destroy the Malayan Union and ensure that the Malays took their proper place in their own land.

But for Dato' Onn's courage and initiative, the country would have been involved in a bloodbath. The very people whom the British had devoted their lives to protect would have become their bitterest most implacable enemies.

In the 4th century BC the Chinese philosopher Lau Tse said, "*Rule a great country as you would cook a small fish. Never make the fire too hot.*" Unfortunately Britain had spoiled its fish by over-cooking. The damage was done, and could not be undone by merely turning back the clock and starting afresh. Time had moved on.

In Britain, the Labour Party had come into power, and tended to reflect the typical 'little Englanders' lack of interest in overseas affairs, even if the new government led by Attlee realised its moral responsibilities and was doing its best to help overseas possessions to achieve independence without breaking friendly connections and mutual assistance.

Events in China itself, where Chiang Kai-shek, the Kuomintang leader, was losing ground to the ultra-Communist Mao Tse-tung, who would soon proclaim the Communist People's Republic, would have far-reaching effects, too. The pro-Communist elements of the Chinese community in Malaya were encouraged to strive for power throughout the while country now the war was over, while in Britain, it quickened the desire to withdraw from Malayan affairs as soon as it was practically possible.

Sir Edward Gent, a courageous and highly-decorated Tank Officer of the First World War (it was said he used to pilot his tank across no-man's land in Flanders by the light of a cigarette) became High Commissioner of the Malayan Union in 1946. But under the tighter reins imposed by Britain's new regime he was little more than a stooge of Whitehall. It was his duty to implement the idealistic schemes that had been cooked up over the Colonial Office gas-fires for Malaya's early independence.

From the moment of his arrival, Sir Edward was stoutly backed by a powerful Chinese Hokkien leader from Malacca. But Tan Cheng Lock was a strong supporter of the Malayan Union, and he warned that if Britain receded in any way from the Union's intentions in so far as they concerned the Chinese he could no longer be held responsible for what they might do. Tan realised that though he could control the Hokkiens he had no power over the Communist Hakkas. It would be the old Hokkien versus Hakka struggle again, this time egged on by Communist China on the one side and democratic Britain on the other. The Malays would side with Britain to oppose the Chinese, and the whole country would be involved (as indeed it was) in an interracial civil war.

Faced with such an appalling dilemma, Gent must have felt that he had no alternative but to carry on with Malaya's enforced and rapid conversion to a Union. Clearly he was actuated more by the realities of the situation than by the Malayan poet Richard Broom's impression that '*With sage advice he recklessly dispenses: UTOPIA! — and damn the consequences!*'

Nevertheless, though acutely aware that order and counter-order must lead to disorder, Whitehall finally came to see that the country was heading for appalling trouble whatever it did.

By continuing with the Malayan Union in the face of the Malays' implacable opposition it was steering the whole country towards certain disaster. No longer was there any hope of giving Malaya back to those who lived there now; it must be returned to those from whom Britain had originally taken it in charge.

Better to have war against Chinese Communists than war against those whom Queen Victoria had placed in Britain's hands. And so, to escape from the embarrassing posture into which it had contorted itself during the trauma of World War II, Whitehall took the only possible course.

It made a complete U-turn.

14. The Emergency: A Long Ordeal

The Malayan Union came to an abrupt end in February 1948, and was replaced by a conception called the Federation of Malaya.

The pendulum had now swung from one extreme to the other. Gone was the free and easy egalitarian system of the pre-war FMS in which everyone had a more or less fair and equal chance. Instead the new Federation of Malaya followed the example of the old Unfederated Malay States. The country's administration was to be in the hands of the Malay half of the community; Islam was to be the national religion, and although machinery was to be devised to hold elections in a democratic fashion, Malayan citizenship conferring the right to vote to would only be granted to those who had passed through a stringent investigation.

Now it was the Chinese who had good cause for complaint. Everything they had been promised was to be taken from them. Had it not been for prospect of the Malayan Union, their sense of disappointment might not have been so great. But to have been granted equality only to have it snatched away was more than they could bear.

Tan Cheng Lok's Council of Joint Action issued direful warnings. Members of the wartime guerrilla forces began to disappear from their work on mines and in rubber estates. As news filtered through that large groups were gathering in the jungle, it became clear that many of these men had prudently left their arms and ammunition hidden in caches when they returned to civilian life after the war. If anger between the entire Chinese population and the Malay people was being deliberately fomented, hatred between the Hokkiens and the Hakkas was rife. In such troubled waters the Communists delighted to fish.

Four months after the collapse of the Malayan Union, war broke out between the Communist-inspired jungle fighters (who were largely Hakka Chinese) and the democratic forces of Malaya and Britain. It was a struggle that was to last for many years and be known, with typical understatement, as The Emergency. And from it the new nation was born.

Initially, it was possible to see some reason for the conflict. But the jungle fighters operations' soon developed into a pattern of pure terrorism and displayed every sign of typical communist aggression, along the lines of similar thrusts (possibly sponsored by China) which were already wreaking havoc in Vietnam, Korea, and other parts of Asia. Their tactics took the shape of infiltration, intimidation, and murder of civilians, in which the law-abiding Chinese peasantry and shopkeepers became the chief and helpless victims.

Slowly the Government came to grips with a menace as lethal and pervasive as a fog of poison gas. Its ability to counter Communist infiltration among labour on the mines and estates, in towns and villages, by brilliant intelligence work; and to cut the lines of supply to the 'bandits' in the jungle, while at the same time winning the support of the people by an imaginative expansion of social services, finally succeeded in defeating the Communist thrust. But it was a total battle — the first and only instance in Asia of outright victory against the forces of Communism.

What eventually brought militant communism to an end in Malaya was the dramatic concept of physically removing a massive proportion of the Chinese agricultural population away from the jungle edges and regrouping them into tighter communities where they could be controlled and guarded. This mass movement of hundreds of thousands of Chinese families needed vast resources of men and money. But it meant that the Hakkas were at last firmly integrated into the country's economy.

Even the aboriginal hill-tribes became involved. There could be no thought of rounding up and resettling these primitive people, who lived by fishing and hunting or burnt off undergrowth to plant a few crops for a season or two and then moved on in an endless circle. Not only would enforced confinement have destroyed their way of life, but whole armies could never have corralled them up. They would merely have merged into the jungle and disappeared like puffs of smoke.

But they were invaluable suppliers of food to the enemy. So gradually a system of jungle forts was devised. Manned by police and army, these strong points were supplied by helicopter with food, medicines and tobacco, all of which were then traded with the jungle folk in exchange for accurate information about the Communist guerrillas' hideouts and general dispositions.

Not only did these tactics prove successful, but they enabled the jungle tribes to become associated with civilised life. Thus, for all its evil, the Emergency was gradually hammering the Malayan peoples into an integrated community.

At first, Sir Edward Gent had stayed on after the downfall of the Malayan Union and might have continued as High Commissioner under the new structure of government had he not been tragically killed in an air crash while flying to London. His place was taken by Sir Henry Gurney, a gentle idealist of leftist leanings, who was to bear the full brunt of the first years of the Emergency.

Though Sir Henry greatly increased the Malayan Police Force with newcomers from Palestine (where he had hitherto served) and called in Colonel Nickol Grey from the Commando branch of the Marines, he was reluctant to accept the realities of outright Communist aggression. Believing that what he saw as a largely local war could be stamped out by efficient police operations, he refused to approve General Briggs' proposals to resettle the Chinese farming population. In return for these well-meaning policies, Sir Henry was held up in a Communist ambush and shot dead.

Meanwhile, the political future of Malaya under the new Federation government was undergoing rapid developments. UMNO had gained strength, and its leader Dato' Onn was trying to promote the growth of inter-racial committees at village level. But external animosities and internal ambitions were too strong for him. When he resigned the leadership and formed a new party, the forward-thrusting UMNO — bent on immediate independence for Malaya — found the man whose stature and temperament was suited to the hour.

So at last appeared the figure of Tunku Abdul Rahman Putra, now known as the Father of Malaya. As the first great leader of Independence, he stands together at this crucial period with the last great figure of the British Empire.

For Sir Winston Churchill, who was once again prime minister, Malaya was full of shocking memories. He felt at home neither with the Far East, nor with the devious methods of Communists which had frustrated and maddened him throughout the war.

But Sir Henry Gurney's murder stung him into action. From Canada, where he was on a visit, he called for the soldier who was next in line for Britain's highest posting as Chief of the Imperial General Staff, and sent him out to Malaya as High Commissioner and Director of Operations combined.

General Sir Gerald Templer arrived like a cold and angry tornado thrashing through the equatorial jungle in 1952. From that moment on, everything was changed. Haphazard commando operations gave way to inspired intelligence work. Malays and Chinese were recruited and trained to act as Home Guards in every village and kampung. Countrywide resettlement of Chinese in accordance with the plan put forward by General Briggs began, insisting that the public should be brought into the battle, whether it was to be told the full truth about the situation, whether it was good news or bad. By means of stringent laws and punishments on the one side, and through vastly improved social services on the other, every person was to be encouraged to join in the struggle.

Above all, Templer ordered that those under his command must get busy and take action. Troops were to move into the jungle and stay there; District Officers were to form executive war committees comprised of military, police, planters and miners; civil heads of departments were to intensify their visits to every corner of their districts and speak up boldly at every central meeting.

Lavish rewards were offered to the public for giving information. Week-long house-curfews were imposed on any town or village where a Communist incident occurred; detention camps were held out to be the only future for irreconciliables. And a commitment was made that Independence would be granted to Malaya as soon as the cancer of Communism had been rooted out.

But most significant of all was the order to regroup the dispersed squatter type of Chinese farmers, and bring them at last into country's administration — a thing which District Officers throughout Malaya had been wanting to do for years.

Huge sums of money were spent on this operation of moving hundreds of thousands of people, which involved purchasing land, planning new villages, providing housing materials, making roads and building police stations, schools, churches, temples, shopping centers, village halls, as well as installing water and providing well-lit perimeter fences around each settlement.

Nor could it have been done without the goodwill and active co-operation of the Chinese farmers themselves. This was achieved partly by paying handsome compensation for the loss of their existing farms and livestock (large instalments were advanced before they moved) and partly by the knowledge that the new locations to which they were going would be of great advantage to the recipients. After all, they had not been living in distant nooks and crannies (or supplying the Communists with food, for that matter) because they liked it, but merely because they had never had a chance to do anything else.

And so they were happy to move. In their new urban surroundings where almost all of them have remained to this day, the resettled Chinese farmers, integrated firmly at last into Malaysia as invaluable residents, are now richer, healthier and better educated than they had ever been before.

For all this, a political solution to Malaya's problems would not have been possible without the presiding genius of Tunku Abdul Rahman Putra, son of a former Sultan of Kedah and now leader of UMNO. Educated at the Penang Free School and Cambridge University, this Malay aristocrat, who in his younger days had been a notable man about town in London and Paris, had a flair for friendship at all social levels, and above all an intuitive sense of timing. He knew exactly what card to play at any moment in the game.

He realised, as so few others did, that the times would not permit Dato' Onn's dream of village communities growing over the years between Malays and Chinese to succeed. He saw that to prepare for the independence Britain was offering it was necessary to forge a political alliance between the various races — Malays, Chinese and Indians — at top leadership level, leaving the ethnic problems in achieving a true Malayan unity to be dealt with later.

While cooperating closely with Sir Gerald Templer to ensure that his party gave the assistance that was needed in forming the Malay

Home Guards, he set about the delicate task of uniting the UMNO leaders with those of the Malayan Chinese Association and the Malayan Indian Congress and creating a spirit of consensus between them that would pave the way for parliamentary government.

At this time the Malayan Communist propaganda had begun to use as its slogan the magic words 'Freedom for Malaya' and astutely Tunku Abdul Rahman turned this slogan to good advantage. He assumed that once Independence had been granted by Britain, the Communist terrorists would be weakened. Their war-cry would then be meaningless as they would have little to offer.

In the long term he was right — though eleven blood-soaked years against the Communists were to pass before the Emergency was officially over. In those wartime conditions, the local population suffered. Miners and planters went to their work in armoured cars and lived behind barbed-wire entanglements but were ambushed and killed in scores (often with their wives and children).

In this long ordeal, the soul of Malaya took on a new unity and came alive. Integrated at last, the new nation of Malaya struggled and was born.

15. The Birth Of A Nation

Fighting side by side with 41 battalions of British troops and supported by the Police Force and 35,000 Home Guards — to say nothing of the military resources of Australia, New Zealand, East Africa and Fiji — the armed forces of Malaya eventually overcame the Communist onslaught. Over 11,000 lives were lost; but this vicious, protracted war constituted Malaya's only real struggle for independence. At no time was there any conflict with Britain. The Emergency (as it continued to be termed, out of deference to the insurance market) was directed jointly by Tunku Abdul Rahman and General Templer; and once it had ceased to be a national menace independence followed as a matter of course.

The Tunku chose 31 August 1957 as the date upon which Malaya's independence would be declared, and three days later the *Agong* (or King) opened the first session of Malaya's new Parliament. Based upon the model of Westminster, it comprised the elected representatives of all the various races of the Malayan population. With Tunku Abdul Rahman as Prime Minister, the new Parliament immediately defined Malaya's position as anti-Communist and anti-neutralist. Malaya joined the Commonwealth and, on the motion of Britain, was elected as a member of the United Nations

Organization. The friendly relations between the two countries were emphasised by a treaty of defence and mutual assistance with Britain, and the appointment of a British general to train and lead the Malayan armed forces. And Malaya was among the first nations to dispatch a battalion of troops to form part of the UN peace-keeping force in the Congo.

Desiring to find a satisfactory solution to its former colonial commitments in Southeast Asia, Britain then won the Tunku's support to the idea of inviting the still-dependent countries of Sabah, Sarawak, Brunei and Singapore to join Malaya in a Federation under his aegis.

However the initial reactions to this suggestion were by no means unanimous. Sabah and Sarawak considered the proposition to be 'totally inoperable at their existing stage of political development' though they were prepared to be merged into one body as a preliminary move. Brunei demurred because of its growing oil wealth and the Sultan's demand to be appointed as Head of the new country.

By contrast, Singapore was almost alarmingly in favour of the new scheme; Lee Kuan Yew's thoughts were perhaps two jumps ahead. But in Malaya itself, UMNO, the leading political party was anxious that it might be 'opening the door of the Peninsula to the Chinese'.

After a series of abortive meetings, the Tunku put forward three compelling reasons for the Federation. Firstly, Britain was determined not to go on acting as caretaker for Southeast Asian defence and administration much longer — she was already under fire from UMNO for trying to hang on to her colonies. Secondly, if Singapore became isolated, there was a danger that the island would become an Asian equivalent of Communist Cuba; and thirdly, if they declined to combine forces, Communism would get them separately, one by one, once Britain departed. His message was clear: they could hang separately if they did not hang together. It was compelling enough to settle the matter; and a Federation of Malaysia, comprising

Malaya, Singapore, Sabah and Sarawak, got off to a shaky start on 17 September 1963.

Almost immediately the new Federation was faced with a revolt in Brunei. Its intention was to seize Sabah and Sarawak and put the Sultan of Brunei on the throne of all three countries, thereby returning to the situation Borneo had been in before the advent of Rajah Brooke and others. At the same time the formation of the Federation provoked violent opposition from Indonesia. So incensed was President Soekarno with the actions taken and the name employed (which he had already earmarked for his own country) that he began a form of armed hostility just short of declared war against Malaya. Confrontation, he called it.

This War of the Running Dogs (as others dubbed it) was a nasty business while it lasted. British and Australian troops — deployed again at Malaysia's request — joined the Malayans in having silent punch-ups with the Indonesians who penetrated the jungles of Borneo along the frontier between Sarawak and Kalimantan. Against a background of vicious anti-Malaysian propaganda, Indonesian units landed on the west coast of Johore, and were parachuted into central areas around Labis. Urban water supplies were poisoned; there were bomb explosions in Singapore.

Such outrages served to exacerbate Sino-Malay tensions, and led to a clash in Singapore known as the Hertogh Riots. During this fracas the police force — which was almost entirely officered and manned by Malays — refused to become involved, and perhaps wisely, remained in its compounds. A less serious, but still ominous, inter-racial clash took place at Bukit Mertajam in Penang. But to cap it all the Singapore-based People's Action Party (PAP) which had been making its presence felt throughout the Malayan peninsula too stridently for the comfort of either UMNO or MCA, suddenly came forward with the slogan: Malaysia for the Malaysians. A seductive warcry! But unhappily one that ran counter to official policy, enshrined in the Constitution which guaranteed the special position of the Malays and a place for all the other races.

At this point Tunku Abdul Rahman showed his calibre as a statesman. Realising the extent of the PAP's influence throughout the country and the support it received in States with large Chinese populations, and knowing the lengths to which the Malays would go if their supremacy was threatened, the Tunku saw that the danger to Malaysia had become too great to be countered by anything but drastic measures. So meeting with Singapore's prime minister, Lee Kuan Yew, on the golf course of the Royal Selangor Club, he suggested that it would be to mutual advantage if Singapore were to leave the Federation and proceed on its own. Somewhat to his surprise, Lee Kuan Yew acquiesced and now conveniently freed from British entanglements, the independent Republic of Singapore was proclaimed. By this initiative a potential bloodbath was averted, and Singapore embarked on her astonishing career.

Meanwhile the problem of semantics had arisen in Malaysia. It is true that no definitive answer exists to the question of the best policy to adopt in a nation composed of several races speaking different languages. For instance, Switzerland and Canada have remained multilingual, whereas the USA has opted to speak English.

In Malaysia the Constitution provides that the national language shall be Malay. At the same time it stated that for a period of ten years or more after Independence, English could be used for all official purposes.

When this ten-year period was about to expire, the Malay-dominated Parliament announced its intention to make Malay the sole official language from 1 September 1967. Whereupon the MCA, upset by this arbitrary decision, put forward demands for a more liberal use of Chinese in government notices and forms.

Hustled by opposing pressures, the Government gave an assurance that the Chinese language would not be sacrificed and appointed a committee to solve the language problem. A bid on behalf of Tamil as well as Chinese was unexpectedly successful , with the result that Parliament passed a Bill agreeing to their use along with English in all government business.

This in turn was greeted with fury by large sections of the Malay community, who regarded such concessions as a betrayal of their cause. Effigies of the revered Tunku were burnt in angry demonstrations. All this was symptomatic of the underlying tensions that still existed in the country. And yet a change was coming over the political texture of Malaysia. Hitherto political parties had been almost entirely base on race; UMNO for the Malays, MCA for the Chinese, MIC for the Indians, Now, two non-racial parties emerged. They were the Democratic Action Party (DAP), a follow-on from the Singapore-based PAP, and the Malaysian People's Movement, known simply as Gerakan. Both were committed to the principles of racial equality; social and economic justice; and parliamentary democracy. But the DAP went further, and called for the immediate implementation of racial equality at all levels and in all fields of national endeavour. Taking exception to the classification of Malaysian citizens as *Bumiputras* and non-*Bumiputras* the DAP tackled head on the bogey of the special position of the Malays which had caused Singapore to leave the Federation and meant that Malaysia was hampered by having to play *Hamlet* without the Prince of Denmark.

In the 1969 General Elections, these two parties made substantial inroads into the majority held by the ruling UMNO/MCA/MIC alliance, capturing Penang and splitting the vote in Perak and Selangor. The election results gave notice that power-brokering between Chinese tycoons and the Malay elite, played to their own private rules, was no longer acceptable to vast numbers of Malaysians. But if the electorate endorsed the idea of a government representing all the races, it nevertheless continued to entertain the notion that

Malay political domination should be maintained, which as the election of course had shown, was a contradiction in terms.

Riots broke out in Selangor when the Chinese held a triumphal procession in Kuala Lumpur, which was attacked by organised bands of UMNO youths. Shots were fired; people were killed, the army was called in. Fortunately the disturbances were confined almost entirely to KL; fortunately too, they acted as a purge to pent-up emotions.

When peace was restored, the Malays realizing that the other races were here to stay, were inclined to be inclined to be conciliatory. Whereas the non-Malay communities understood that under the circumstances they had better make do with what they had got.

At all events, the Agong took matters in hand with commendable speed. Declaring a state of emergency, he prorogued Parliament, appointed a National Operations Council chaired by the Deputy Prime Minister, Tun Abdul Razak, and promulgated a series of necessary but restrictive laws regulating public actions and attitudes. It speaks volumes for the newly-pacific attitude of more than half the Malaysian population that not a murmur was uttered.

After enacting a number of forceful measures, such as assembling a form of Home Guard to ensure domestic peace between the various races, and setting up a profusion of goodwill committees, the National Operations Council disbanded and the country returned to normal. If anything, conditions were improved; at least people knew where they were.

One result of this regrettable incident was that Tunku Abdul Rahman, having shouldered the burden of attaining independence for Malaysia, retired from politics.

16. Penang's Progress

At the time of Independence, George Town was still quite a small but exceptionally beautiful port of some 300,000 inhabitants, nearly all of whom were long-resident Hokkien Chinese of British nationality.

Its ambience was unique. Against the background of wooded mountains and a placid seascape, the minaret of an occasional mosque jutted gracefully up into the cool blue air from an expanse of red-tiled Chinese roofs and white colonial facades. The town itself was made up of narrow, shaded alleys lined with yellow-painted walls and attractively curved gable-ends; fine old trees bordered open spaces of well-kept grass, where Chinese and English cricketers in white flannels lounged in the shade through drowsy afternoons. Though long outpaced by its great business rival, Singapore, Penang remained a rich and busy maritime entrepot serving the northern half of Malaya, whereas Singapore catered for the southern part from Kuala Lumpur down.

Once the Japanese War was over, life gradually returned to normal and went on much the same as before, except for the presence of large numbers of American soldiers who came down from Indo-China on leave. They stayed at the E&O Hotel and in the few other caravanserais that George Town then possessed. As yet there were no high-rise buildings, nor indeed any hint of urban sprawl — what we now term satellite development.

If a system of zoning had always been firmly maintained throughout the township to preserve the amenities of the shopping, business and residential districts in European fashion, no regulation existed for any sort of racial segregation in the town planning. But the well-to-do members of the community of whatever race, tended to live in massive villas with large gardens in what the Municipality called 'A' zones, that is along Logan Road, Kelawei Road, Northam Road, and so forth. On the other hand, the clerical and artisan population of Malays and Muslim-Indians for the most part clustered round their mosques at Kampong Dodol, Tanjong Tokong and Tanjong Bungah; while the Hindu Indians inhabited the Waterfall and Gottlieb Road areas, or out towards Ayer Itam at the foot of Penang Hill.

Whether desperately poor manual workers or opulent capitalists, the Chinese, who comprised a majority of the urban population, did everything and lived everywhere — from overcrowded rooming houses in back alleys to marvellous palaces on Northam Road. Present day visitors from overseas often remark upon the splendid mansions along George Town's avenues and hint that the old colonials used to do themselves pretty well. But if by that they mean the British, they are making a mistake. Every one of these stately dwellings with its handsome carriage-drive and spacious lawns was built by some Chinese tycoon, many of whom had worked their way up from pulling a rickshaw. (And good luck to them, too.)

No, the British lived more modestly, often in company houses in the general area of the Residency, along Western, Brown and Scott Roads, or near the old racecourse. (Though they came into their own up at the hill village of Strawberry, where before the war the entire summit — excluding the village itself — was reserved for expatriates' dwellings.)

Elsewhere outside town, Wearne's small airstrip down at Bayan Lepas in the south of the island was enlarged sufficiently in 1947 to take a regular service of Malaya's inter-state commercial aircraft — the forebears of both MAS and Singapore Airlines. While up to the north at Batu Ferringhi a small single-storey hotel with a few rooms, called the Lone Pine, came into being to cater for weekend swimmers.

At the time this may have seemed a hazardous enterprise, since apart from the local Malays no one but Europeans ever thought of venturing into the sea. But as a matter of fact, an astonishing change was coming over the predilections of Penang. For gradually the empty beaches of soft golden sand began to be filled with picnic parties and bathers of all races (positively congested, muttered the old-timers, if they spotted anyone within a couple of hundred yards). Indeed the young Chinese, with their fine physiques, proved themselves to be excellent swimmers; and soon water polo, sailing (and later surfboard sailing) together with every form of sport from tennis and golf to mountain climbing and jungle exploration, began to fill the lives of the island's young people. Badminton and soccer were especially popular.

This spirit of change — or, if you prefer, emergence of an affluent consumer-oriented middle class — became evident in the late Fifties when a few suburban bungalows in their own gardens sprang up around Tanjong Tokong, Tanjong Bungah and Hillside; and a smart new residential area called Jesselton grew up on rising land near the turf club. Moreover to the south, down the narrow tree-lined road that led to Gelugor and on to the airport, a large coconut plantation was chopped down to make way eventually for a complete satellite town of modest but attractive terrace-type dwellings for the rapidly growing numbers of young business and professional families. In addition to these developments, which were chiefly carried out by private enterprise, the Municipality undertook a large low-cost housing scheme at the old golf-course near Gelugor with finance loaned by the Federal government; and when a German firm obtained the contract to build the first agglomeration of prefabricated, multi-storeyed blocks of flats near the rifle-range at the foot of the hill, the outline of George Town began perceptibly, indeed dramatically to alter.

Yet temperamentally many people in Penang viewed the prospect of their old colonial Straits Settlements being merged into the new nation of Malaya without much enthusiasm. They had no desire to lose their status as subjects of Britain with all the benefits that implied. In the run-up to Independence there was a good deal of barely concealed disquiet among the Chinese community leaders who foresaw that such a change would inevitably spell the end of the Settlements' hitherto predominant position. However these misgivings were to some extent placated by visits and reassurances from various members of Parliament who were sent out from London and the Independence celebrations went off in Penang without incident, albeit with but modest demonstrations of joy. After all, with their British nationality, their cricket and a way of life inherited from five generations, many Penang Chinese felt that they were almost a county of England, rather than a colony.

However, being a highly civilised place, Penang was prepared to accept in good part whatever destiny decreed.

In fact during the first few years of Independence the island's progress was slow but steady, as it tried to find its feet in the new situation. Municipal works in George Town carried on with the schemes that had already been dawn up. A new road was constructed between Ayer Itam and Bayan Lepas to serve as a secondary access to the airport and provide for a mid-island highway across to the western plain and village of Balik Pulau, while at the same time acting as the starting point for an agricultural road up to Strawberry on the top of Penang Hill. Work continued on the pre-war project of installing water-borne sewerage out of the old part of George Town — a difficult operation carried out with great expertise. The first steps were taken to improve Penang's water supply by building a large reservoir up in the hills behind Ayer Itam village; and put a stop to the projected touristic highway up the hill, an extravaganza which was making more landslips than progress and ruining the north of the island's ecology. Finally, once the British military presence which had been retained by the Malayan government after Independence was no longer considered necessary, the handsome Minden Barracks built during the wars on David Brown's old property at Gelugor, were handed over to the Ministry of Education to become a site for a new college, not far from the Universiti Sains Malaysia, founded in the 1970s.

If initially the MCA had been the most important political force in the State of Penang, it was not long before the Gerakan came into power. With its policy based on non-communal and non-racial lines, it was more suitable in a multi-racial State, though opposed by many Malays in Province Wellesley and those living in the island's western plain.

Clearly, if it were not to find itself isolated and starved out of funds from the central government in Kuala Lumpur, Gerakan had to join the Federal alliance. This called for some careful manipulation — one might almost say horse-trading — and the price it had to pay for admittance was the loss of the free port status that had ensured Penang's predominance as a leading entrepot for the previous 175 years.

But the people running Penang were nothing if not pragmatic. Faced with this predicament, they came up with two alternatives: industrial development and tourism.

To implement these objectives, a quasi-governmental body called the Penang Development Corporation (PDC) was formed which gazetted two large customs-free industrial zones, one in

Province Wellesley and the other near the airport at Bayan Lepas. Both were destined solely for the assembly and export of finished products produced from raw or unfinished materials sent in from abroad and completed by local labour. The scheme worked so well that it has materially contributed to the State's finances, while ensuring that there was no problem of unemployment in Penang.

Apart from this, the PDC also undertook to assist private enterprise in every way possible to develop the whole island, especially in Batu Ferringhi, into a tourist resort. As a result, foreign investors flocked in and the Lone Pine was no longer alone. For soon a glittering array of luxury hotels in manicured gardens appeared, to give the northern beaches a Riviera flavour — one has only to think of the Polynesian-styled Rasa Sayang and the Golden Sands, which are all operated by the great Shangri-La hotel chain; the Holiday Inn; the former Casuarina (a joint enterprise started by Swissair, Nestlé and local interests, now about to become the Hard Rock Penang) and the imposing Bayview Beach Resort with its lovely gardens overlooking the famous rock, let alone the Mutiara further along the bay at Teluk Bahang, to appreciate the new international ambience that Batu Ferringhi has acquired. The descendants of the Malay refugees from the Siamese invasion of long ago now find employment catering for the hordes of tourists who come in each year from all parts of the world, and Penang has become a household word in the vocabulary of travel.

The PDC also sponsored an enormous housing scheme to the south of George Town, which involved the creation of a complete new township on the way to the airport. Although Bayan Baru was originally intended to house workers in the Bayan Lepas customs-free zone, it quickly attracted people from the town who preferred to commute in transport provided by their employers; with the result that its inhabitants are mostly junior civil servants (who receive special housing grants) as well as young members of the business community.

Indeed the success of Bayan Baru foreshadowed a tidal wave of speculative building by private entrepreneurs, many from as far away as Hong Kong, and often with scant regard for orderly planning. Moreover high-rise condominiums with swimming pools on their roofs and garages for hundreds of cars underneath, to say nothing of towering office blocks constructed of coloured glass, began to bulge over the little streets below and dwarf the remnants of gracious old Penang. A structural dream of the future in the shape of the sixty-eight storey KOMTAR emerged in the very middle of the town. Said to have been the first construction of its kind in Southeast Asia, it was intended to be a center point where everybody who mattered would be in touch with each other, though there were some who felt that this ivory tower was in danger of cutting its inmates off from reality.

Certainly it takes vision and courage to interpret the needs of a world that is diminishing in distances yet increasing in population, and if the current world wide depression has lately been striking at the roots of this shiny new nation at least the spade work has been done to confront the challenges of the 21st century. What's more, enormous progress has been achieved in health, education, interracial harmony, and with so many other factors which contribute to the welfare of the citizens in Malaysia.

Yet though Penang is now linked to the mainland by the longest bridge in the East — and through Malaysia itself to the countries in ASEAN — it continues to remain in many impalpable ways the same bewitching and individual island that it has always been: a tropical jewel in its glorious setting, a stimulating social climate to live in and indeed to visit.

On 7 July 2008, the UNESCO World Heritage Committee, meeting at Quebec, declared George Town a World Heritage Site.

Jointly described (with Malacca) as The Historic Cities of the Straits of Malacca, the UNESCO citation goes on to describe them as '...a unique architectural and cultural townscape without parallel anywhere in East and Southeast Asia.'

Sitting on the rock at Batu Ferringhi, you have only to cast your mind back over its history, and breathe in the invigorating atmosphere of today, to know that this is so.

Part Two

Penang: Its Peoples

The Hidden Heritage of the Penang Malays

So far, we've only touched briefly on the rich and varied heritage of the Malays in Penang. It is clear that a few indigenous Malays have lived on the island for a long time. The beachside villagers were probably settlers or descendants of those who had been sent by the Sultans of Kedah to keep watch for naval expeditions from Siam, which claimed suzerainty over the northern Malay states; whereas the 'naked Indians' described by Lancaster were probably Semang-Pangan aborigines or *orang asli*. There were also a number of Indonesians around, whose marriages to native Malay women led to padi-planting villages. Their descendants slowly absorbed the aborigines whose last settlement at Kubang Semang disappeared in the 1920s. Penang's last padi field still exists at Kampung Seronok near the airport.

It was Sultan Ahmad Tajuddin, himself of West Sumatran Minangkabau stock, who granted permission to the three royal Nakhoda brothers to settle in Penang. Between them, the trio had charge over what is now Bayan Lepas, Balik Pulau, Gelugor and modern-day Georgetown. Nakhoda Intan, founded Penang's oldest mosque at Batu Uban; and his grave is now a *keramat* or Malay shrine. His descendants include Malaysia's first minister of agriculture, Aziz Ishak, and Singapore's first president, Yusuf Ishak.

When Francis Light finally obtained the island, it was with the help of these early Malay and other settlers that he built the first Fort Cornwallis. In those days, it was little more than a stockade of palm and *nibong* tree trunks. Light certainly recognised the importance of the Malays, even if his extensive shipping records failed to count their small, light boats. The first Superintendent listed only ships of 50 tons (50,000kg) or more. Records of the visits of smaller Malay boats (there were at least nine different categories of them, based on size and origin) were haphazard. By 1792, close on 200 of these smaller craft were sailing into Penang's waters, and the following year more than a thousand large Malay vessels were making the same journey regularly.

Most of these traders brought only one kind of product. Yet the items transported in their individual boats ranged from tin, gold, rice, sago, spices, textiles and salt to tobacco, birds' nests, rattan and betel nuts. Bugis textiles were extensively traded, and Indian cloth was especially prized.

Through his own Indonesian connections, Light persuaded influential Achinese to move to Penang. One of these, Tunku Syed Hussain, eventually controlled the southern part of Georgetown where he built the *Gedong Acheh* (the island's first high-rise building). It still stands, though locals refer to it as the *Rumah Tinggi*, meaning the tall house. A four-storey building, it served as a market place for spices from his homeland. Syed Hussain, a noted philanthropist, lived and was finally laid to rest at Acheen Street (Lebuh Acheh), where so many of his countrymen set up homes that the entire street was named after them. The mosque he founded in 1808 is probably the only one with swallow-tail roof ridges, evidence of a Chinese Muslim influence.

Until the early nineteenth century, most Malay arrivals were either Bugis or Achinese. Quite a few had Arab origins. Among these were highly educated descendants of the Badridzwan and

Bafadal *qabilah* (clans) that became Qadis and Muftis, propagating the Islamic faith even as they built up their business holdings. They used the small Pinang River to transport their goods and built the *Masjid Lama* (old mosque) *Sungei Pinang* along its banks.

Descendants of other Indonesian free settlers who married local Malay women were known as Jawi Peranakan (shortened to *Jawi Pekan* in typically laissez-faire Penang fashion because they all lived in towns). Also called Straits Malays, their legacy includes the *boria*, a popular form of choral singing distinct to Penang, and *bangsawan*, elaborate street operas.

Others came to Penang under less happy circumstances. So many slave boys and girls, mostly from Bali, Nias, Toba and Karo, were sold at Tanjong Tokong that a short Malay poem still commemorates the fact:

Tanjong Tokong tanah merah,
Anak dara murah-murah,
Satu dua duit saja.

Tanjong Tokong the red land,
(where) Virgins are cheap,
One for two cents only.

The British banned slavery. But they could not stop the (mainly) rich Chinese owners from surreptitiously procuring a supply of these intelligent, fair-skinned Malay youngsters, whom they found so attractive that some of the kindlier ones made their new slaves lesser wives or concubines. These girls became the matriarchs of numerous Peranakan Cina or Penang Straits-Chinese families.

Since the early part of the 19th century, Penang was also the transit point for the *haj* pilgrimage to Mecca. Pak Ma'sum Mendeleng (a Mandailing from Indonesia) ran it so successfully that it became a small industry of its own. Later, control passed into the hands of the al-Mashoor family who came from Arabia. These pilgrim brokers, who were all called Sheikh Haji as a sign of respect (there was one for almost every Malay community), carried on until the 1970s when the *haj* ships were replaced by aeroplanes and the national Pilgrimage Board (*Tabung Haji*) vessels. Tengku Tjhik di Tiro, one of the fiercest opponents of the Dutch colonisers, set off to perform the *haj* from Penang in the 1850s.

Many Indonesians were chafing under the harsh rule of their Dutch masters. Thus when the Dutch attacked Acheh in 1873, prominent Penang Malays supported the Achinese resistance. Syed Mohamed Alatas, a much-respected philanthropist, led the Muslim secret society known as the *Bendera Merah* (Red Flag) and smuggled arms to them from his mansion at the junction of Armenian Street. Built around 1860, this former base of revolutionary operations with its Indian, Malay, Chinese and European architectural features fully restored, currently houses the Penang Islamic Museum.

Indonesian exiles, who successfully found refuge on the island, formed the Council of Eight (*Dewan Delapan*). Mohammad Samin Thayeb, a leader of the seminal Sarekat Islam movement in Sumatra, Makaluddin Nasution, Halalloedin Hamzah (who was of Mandailing descent) also came over. To avoid detection, Halalloedin, who wrote incendiary articles for *Pewarta Deli* and *Kompas*, changed his name to Ahmad Noor Abdul Shukoor, while Tan Malaka, the famous Indonesian nationalist, had to dress up as a Chinese. He found refuge at Samin Thayeb's Chulia Street shop, from whence he sailed for Belawan on one of the latter's ships.

Penang's artistic and literary connection with Indonesia probably has some roots in this revolutionary movement. National Laureate Dato' Abdullah Hussain was so involved in the fight for Indonesian independence that he was one of the special Malaysian guests at their golden jubilee celebrations. Many of the island's leading Malay journalists were trained by the press in Medan. The best pre-war Malay novel — the first to have a Malayan setting — was written by Ahmad Rashid Talu, who was extensively published in Indonesia, while in Malayan music and cinema the name P. Ramlee stands out. Singer, script writer, actor, songwriter, director and recording artiste, Penang's favourite son won awards in Tokyo, Taipei and Hong Kong. Few modern Malaysians know that his real name was Teuku Zakariah bin Teuku Nyak Puteh. The great P. Ramlee, a former Free School boy, was the son of an Achinese sailor.

It wasn't strange that a Malaysian cultural icon should have been English-educated. Originally Malay education began in small huts with Arab or Arab-trained missionaries preaching and teaching (princes and the sons of wealthy men had private tutors). But with the other races learning English as a means of advancement, it became imperative for Malay boys be able to speak and write the language well if they were not to be left behind. Forward-looking Malays began sending their children to the English schools set up by the Catholic and Protestant (usually Anglican) missionaries. The list of alumni at Penang Free School, St. Xavier's Institution, Convent Light Street, St. George's and Convent Pulau Tikus, have as many famous Malay names as European, Chinese and Indian ones.

The learning of English, especially at Christian schools, was a sensitive issue. While speaking to *The Star*, former Malaysian prime minister Tun Dr. Mahathir recalled about his father, Mohamad Iskandar, "My father was one of the few Malays who went to school then. He was so passionate about learning that he went to school without telling his parents because they did not want him to go to a mission school in Penang."

Mohamad Iskandar encountered many obstacles learning and subsequently teaching English. He was the only Malay providing an English education to members of the Kedah royalty and the elite circles in which they moved — one of his students was Tunku Abdul Rahman, Malaysia's first prime minister and the Father of Independence. It was only a matter of time before the far-sighted Sultan Abdul Hamid invited him to move to Alor Star as the first headmaster of the Sultan Abdul Hamid College.

The rich variety of Penang's Malay heritage slipped from sight when Malaya began its own struggle for self-rule. Muslims in Malaysia banded together as Malays irrespective of their origins. Indian Muslims (affectionately known as *mamaks*), Arabs, Mandailings, Achinese, Bugis, all became Malays — a fact that makes it almost impossible for many to trace back their lineage beyond the Second World War. The extent of this ethnic unity is reflected in the fact that a modern Penang Malay family might have members with Arab, Chinese, Indian, Thai, Indonesian or even Eurasian features.

It became even harder to define the Penang Malay when free trade and industrial zones were opened up during the 1970s and Malays from other less-developed states flocked to the island and Province Wellesley to seek employment in the new factories. They quickly made new homes and lives for themselves. By 2000, the Malays had become the largest community in the state of Penang, making up 60% of the population while Chinese numbers fell to about 30%.

Such diversity notwithstanding, the original Malay culture and customs are still evident. For example, the *sarung* is worn by men and women of all races while *sambal belacan* (fish paste pounded with fresh chilli pods) has made its way into every kitchen. The Malay practice of holding *kenduri* or open house parties for the whole village has become an institution practised by Buddhists, Christians and Hindus at Chinese New Year, Christmas and Deepavali.

The sharing of language and culture has not been all one way. The languages spoken in Penang, including English, are liberally sprinkled with Malay words (sometimes comically mispronounced by non-Malays) while Penang Malays are known to speak or at least understand a fair bit of Hokkien (the most common Chinese dialect) or Tamil. Penang Malay cuisine, too, influenced by long association with Indonesians, Indians, Chinese, Thai and yes, even the British, is considered to be the best if not necessarily an authentic form of Malay cooking.

Perhaps the most nostalgic reminder of the great Malay heritage in Penang is *nasi lemak* — a simple dish comprising a bowl of rice cooked in coconut milk, with a dab of sweet and sour anchovy or prawn curry and half a boiled egg on top. It was originally a snack but the innovative Penang mentality (not to mention pretentious restaurants and hotels) slowly elevated it to a complete meal with twenty or thirty side-dishes.

Still, it isn't too hard to imagine a Malay housewife carefully wrapping the *nasi* in a banana leaf, all ready for her husband to eat in the padi field three or four hundred years ago.

The Chinese in Penang

Francis Light could not possibly have foreseen that Khoh Lee Wan and his followers were just the tip of the Chinese iceberg. Not even when he remarked in a dispatch (1794) that '*the Chinese were the most numerous and hardworking settlers*' on the island. So many were busily making new lives as '*traders, carpenters, masons, planters and merchants*' that there was a thriving industry importing, cooking and selling their favourite foods from home. They even had a self-help secret society, the Ghee Hin, which went on to acquire a more martial role in local affairs. But the great majority of Chinese were not particularly interested in politics, except when it affected their ability to make money. They kept to themselves; only their Kapitan had much to do with the British authorities.

As the colonial economies in Malaya and Indonesia grew, more and more Chinese came. They arrived with nothing but dreams of a better life, and more money through hard work. Whatever these *sinkeh* (new guests) could spare, they sent back to their families in China. The Chinese Protectorate Report of 1881 mentioned that the *sinkeh* worked for 360 days a year, for which their new employers fed them and paid them $30 to $48, of which $18 to $20 per annum was deducted for their passage. They also received a mosquito net, a bamboo hat, two pairs of breeches, two towels and a pair of wooden clogs *gratis*. Those that ended up in Indonesia were indentured to Dutch masters who treated them like slaves. Every man was carefully identified to the extent of being measured in case he tried to run away from a harsh life that included constant beatings and whippings. Not surprisingly, they described themselves as coolies (from *ku* and *li* the Chinese words for sorrow and strength) — a word that has entered the English lexicon.

The Penang *sinkeh* enjoyed better lives and opportunities under their more benevolent English masters. As early as 1819, Lim Seong Pan and Khoo Beng San had the distinction of being listed in the *Prince of Wales Island Directory* as Chinese merchants. Relations between the Chinese and the British were generally cordial and cooperative. Sir George Leith, for example, was so highly regarded that when his term of office ended, the Kapitan gave a testimonial speech in which he called Sir George '*a father to all ranks*.' They named a street after him, too. Perhaps his generosity had something to do with it. In 1801, Kapitan Hu Shiming (or Terqua) acquired a perpetual title from Leith (one of a hundred the Lieutenant-Governor handed out that day) for a piece of land at King Street which became the location of many of the island's most influential associations. Even the Penang Riots of 1867 were due to Chinese secret society disputes between the Cantonese-speaking Ghee Hin and the Hakka Hai San, and not resentment against the British. Of course the colonial administration played a policing and peacekeeping role in these skirmishes — Cannon Street was named to commemorate the cannons and iron balls they shot into the Chinese enclave.

Perhaps Khoh Lee Wan (*Che* or Mister Wan to the Malays) can take some credit for sparking off the dreams of all the Chinese who flocked to Penang. He was so successful that his great-grandson, Seang Tat, became the first Penang merchant to obtain the opium and spirit rights for Singapore in 1880. This enterprising young man built a magnificent mansion which he named Edinburgh House after the Duke stayed with him in 1869. Seang Tat went on to serve as Municipal Councillor and Justice of the Peace. Another great-grandson, Hong Beng, was adopted by Forbes Brown, a British planter, before studying at the University of Edinburgh. Reputed to have a superb command of English, Chinese, French and German, he wrote *The Spirit of Chinese Civilization* which was highly praised by European academics, and was.

There were tin, rubber, opium and spirits millionaires — for a number of years, the revenue from opium alone accounted for 49% of Straits Settlements revenue) and there were sugar tycoons such as Khaw Boo Aun, who was not only a Justice of the Peace but also the only Asian Commissioner in the British *Commission of Enquiry into the State of Labour in The Straits Settlement and the Native States*. A different Khaw, a vegetable gardener named Soo Cheang, built up his humble plot of land into a trade and mining empire covering so much of south-western Thailand that the King of Siam appointed him governor of Ranong. His second son inherited this title; his sixth son, Khaw Sim Bee, became governor of Trang, Kanburi and Phuket. Through his various companies, their House of Ranong (*Na Ranong* in the Thai kingdom) acquired extensive interests in shipping. Khaw's Khean Guan Insurance Company pioneered the insurance business in Malaya. The only public monument dedicated to a Chinese businessman in Thailand still stands in Trang today.

But it wasn't just these early *arrivistes* that made themselves millionaires. Loh Boon Siew, still remembered as a philanthropist in Malaysia, Singapore, Thailand, Indonesia and China, came off the boat at the start of the Great Depression of 1929. He was 13 years old, illiterate, and a few ragged clothes in an old cardboard case was the sum of his worldly possessions. By the time he died in 1994, his vast holdings stretched from Penang and China across the Pacific to Australia and New Zealand.

But before Boon Siew, the Big Five (the Tan, Yeoh, Lim, Cheah and Khoo families) had extensive tin, rubber, opium, coconut oil, sugar, rice and spirit co-partnerships with the English and even some Armenians. They extended their interests from Penang to Thailand, some Dutch Indonesian territories, as well as China, Japan, Burma, and Siberia. They were the primary suppliers of Chinese goods like crockery, salted foodstuffs, mats, rice noodles and clothes (iron woks, too). In the three years preceding 1842, more than 800,000 pieces of crockery were sent from Penang to Burma in their ships.

In those days, however, the Chinese still regarded themselves as guests in a foreign land. They wore the pigtail as a sign that their political loyalties lay in China, even if the base of their commercial interests was firmly rooted in the Straits Settlements. Among them were a number of Manchu-appointed Chinese Vice-Consuls, while those who could afford to do so hedged their bets by purchasing various grades of civil or military titles from the Qing government. Admittedly, this was more for show than anything else since they had nothing to do with the Manchu imperial court in Beijing.

But when the Chinese nationalist, Sun Yat-sen, needed help for the 1911 Revolution, Penang's tycoons, traders and coolies were unstinting in their contributions. The great reformer lived in Georgetown for a time. His old office at 120, Armenian Street was the base of the *Tongmenhui* party which was instrumental in transforming China into a republic. This nondescript two-storey shophouse also housed the Penang Philharmonic Union and the first modern Chinese newspaper in the world, the *Kwong Hwa Jit Poh*, which Sun founded on 20 December 1910.

There is some argument about whether the historic Penang Conference on 13 November 1910 was actually held there or at

404 Jalan Datuk Keramat since Sun conducted revolutionary meetings at a number of other buildings in Penang. But there is no doubt his eloquence raised enough funds to finance the Second Guangzhou Uprising. These donations were so vital to the success of the revolt, that Sun Yat-sen himself recognised the Overseas Chinese as the Mother of the Revolution.

Despite their loyalty to their homeland, important events in Britain were celebrated just as faithfully in Penang. Queen Victoria's Diamond and George V's Silver Jubilees were commemorated with processions, decorated arches, and floats; as were the Prince of Wales' visit and the coronations of George VI and Elizabeth II. The Chinese Chamber of Commerce had its own golden stagecoach pulled by eight horses for such occasions.

Not surprisingly, the Chinese were granted a free hand in many matters. They built numerous temples, whose committees frequently served as arbiters of communal matters. With 10 directors each from the two largest dialectical groups, the Goddess of Mercy Temple at Pitt Street was the supreme authority in Chinese internal affairs for many years until the Chinese Town Hall was built in 1881. However, a Chinese Protectorate had been set up in 1877, and later an Advisory Board was formed with a British Chairman who sat with the representatives of each dialectical group. The Penang Chinese Chamber of Commerce was founded in 1903. It remains one of the strongest commercial institutions in Malaysia. But the ever practical Chinese also set up self-help societies based on surnames, places of origin, dialect, employment or craft — among the oldest being the guild of master carpenters (1855). Even the apprentices had one, and, considering Penang's reputation as a gourmand's paradise, it was inevitable that the tea houses and restaurants should have their own venerable guild, established in 1875.

The Chinese had their own schools too (though not a few tried to send at least one son to the elite Penang Free School to learn

English) and they were allowed to make their businesses as large and profitable as they could. Messrs. Tiang, Lee & Co. for instance, were a six-merchant cabal that became one of the first Chinese companies to deal directly with the Americans and Europeans, while Quah Beng Kee introduced the first ferry service between the island and Province Wellesley on the mainland. Chinese millionaires and their English-style mansions sprang up everywhere — Cheah Chen Eok, the Superintendent of the Penang Opium and Spirit Farm Syndicate, for example, passed his days either in a grand country house with magnificently scrolled wrought iron gates at Coombe Hill or his other equally impressive home, Edgecombe, on Penang Hill.

All Chinese, no matter how rich or poor, were free to indulge their favourite vices. Apart from opium, gambling helped to keep many coolies destitute. Pleasures of the flesh were so easily available that by the 1920s, Campbell Street (still notorious as a red light area in the 1960's) had 38 brothels and 760 registered prostitutes. Indeed a Penang Cabaret Women's Association was established to protect the rights of taxi dancers — ladies who danced with men for a fee. Any other services they offered were never mentioned. It was the heyday of the genteel westernized oriental, after all. Ironically, the *Po Leung Kuk Home* which was set up to protect girls below 16 years of age from the oldest profession, eventually became a byword for housing bad girls. Chinese mothers used to threaten to send their young daughters to the home if they misbehaved.

But back then, such things were taken much more lightly. Even the secret societies were regarded in a more kindly light. In 1854, the head of the Ghee Hin secret society was held in such high respect that he could quite openly, and amid much fanfare in the community, donate a piece of land for the Pauper Hospital for mendicants and opium addicts (the British only built the General Hospital in 1882). When the society was dissolved in 1890, it wound up its affairs in a manner which modern business conglomerates would do well to follow: monies were equitably distributed, properties were sold or transferred to trusted members and arrangements were made for prayers to be held in perpetuity at the society's temple. (They still are.)

When Japan invaded China just before WWII, the British allowed the Penang Chinese to form a number of societies to provide aid for their mainland relatives. But once the Japanese were in control, they were smart enough to capitalize on the situation, forcing the Penang Oversea-Chinese Association to raise $7 million in voluntary donations. Perhaps because of this, the colonial government kept a close eye on these associations, to the extent of screening speeches, plays and songs performed to raise funds, though it must be stressed that quite a few Chinese men and women chose to serve with the British army in China, India and Burma. Yet inevitably, a Communist Party of Malaya sprang up. It collaborated with British intelligence throughout the conflict, until the unavoidable split came and the movement was driven underground. Its members carried on their lonely war until the turn of the millennium, when they finally gave up the struggle.

Not just ideological differences between communism and capitalism divided the Chinese community. Never missing an opportunity for financial advancement, many Chinese realised that a knowledge of English was the quickest way up for them. Those who could afford it had their children tutored in the language, and sent off to further their studies in Britain as soon as they could. This wasn't really a new idea. As early as 1898, the Viceroy of Guangdong and Hunan, Huang Zhidong, with the lessons of the Sino-French War still fresh in mind, had promulgated the doctrine of 'Chinese learning as the fundamental of structure, Western learning for practical application.'

The Straits-Chinese, especially, embraced the idea so fervently that they came to be known as the Queen's Chinese. Descendants of inter-marriage with the Malays, they stood a little apart from the rest of the community with their mix of cultural practices and curiously poetical *patois* — a combination of English, Hokkien and Malay. At first they were as anxious to retain their cultural roots as they were to understand and profit from their association with the Europeans. Chan Kim Boon got his English education at the Penang Free School but was privately tutored in Chinese, for example. He went on to pioneer Baba (the colloquial term for Straights-Chinese men) literature, translating classical Chinese fiction into the Baba-Malay dialect.

With their adoption of western and especially English ways, it was inevitable that *Nyonyas* (their daughters) were soon joining their brothers at universities in Europe. The results were considered mixed blessings. For instance, what must the old-timers have thought when their sons got married in European suits instead of Qing-style clothes and bowl caps? Brides took a little longer to discard their flower crowns and scarlet garments for white gowns and lacy veils — this would have shocked the traditionally educated Chinese most of all, since white robes used to be worn at funerals.

There was no holding back the dictates of fashion then as now. When funeral customs — probably the penultimate bastion of the old ways — came under siege, the loss of interest in the traditional way of life caused a split between those that went to English schools and those who attended Chinese institutions. Politicians with an eye on the Chinese vote have to step warily in this minefield of communal sensitivities.

The only common grounds that remain, it seems, are the love of making money — and food. On that, all Chinese remain firmly united in the belief that the best — be they time-honoured hawker specialities or the sweet, sour and very spicy *Nyonya* cuisine — is to be found only in Penang.

Penang's Indian Connection

When Francis Light made his daring flit from Kuala Kedah to Penang, one of the passengers was probably Alaudin Meerah Hussein Lebai, a Chulia from South India, who went on to found the Ariffin Mosque and the Mesjid Kongsi (i.e. shared or communal mosque). There is evidence, moreover, of an earlier Indian presence. A shrine at Datuk Keramat, possibly dating back to 1715, is said to have belonged to a Malabari named Sangli Perappa or Fakir Melana. Certainly, merchants from the Indian sub-continent had been in the archipelago since the earliest days of the spice trade. They ran a profitable line in precious metals and textiles and were a major force in the heyday of the Malaccan empire (1456–1511).

Yet it is generally agreed that the real exodus to Penang began with the establishment of the British trading port. Enterprising Indians began moving in from other Malay states, followed by more from Acheh and Borneo. By 1794, as many as 2,000 Indian men were making a bee-line to Penang; even so their numbers simply weren't enough to carry out Light's grand plans.

The Superintendent had to make his new bailiwick profitable. His offers of free grants of land soon attracted other British traders and cash crop plantations began springing up all over the isle. Some

Chinese took up sugar-cane and pepper farming but the majority were more interested in tin mining. Since there were still too few Malays on the island to make a go of it, another source of reliable, hardworking labourers was urgently required.

The abjectly poor and down-trodden Adi Dravidas who barely grubbed enough to feed themselves, were just what was needed. And they came in droves. *Kappalu* (Indian ships) embarked for Penang with their living cargoes from a number of ports along the Malabar and Coromandel coasts. The minute they arrived, these new workers were met and whisked off to the plantations. Later quite a few were sent to work in Province Wellesley and Perak.

Though few people know it nowadays, the British also deported to Penang and Singapore those Indian convicts who had been sentenced to more than seven years imprisonment. When the first boatload arrived in 1790, the prisoners were put to work and trained in various trades. The Malabari convicts, especially, were reputed to have built most of the government buildings, and were responsible for the fine plaster work and masonry in the best Muslim homes. They enjoyed greater freedom than the Chinese convicts later transported from Hong Kong, because the authorities knew that there were no Indian secret societies that might help them to escape.

Unlike the Chinese coolies, Indian labourers were contracted for only two or three years at a time. Their main aim was to save enough money to make a better life for their families at home. Coming from harsh, impoverished backgrounds, their needs were simple and their vices few. They lived inside the plantations, in communal quarters provided by the owners. Food was cheap and plentiful; their more enterprising brothers were quick to set up little food shops near these large communities of married bachelors. The agricultural work came easily to them after their years of backbreaking toil in India. They also had the freedom to worship wherever and whenever they wanted; neither Light nor any of their predominantly British employers practised religious discrimination. Compared to back home, life in Penang must have seemed almost cushy.

By the beginning of the 1800s' large numbers of Tamils were also being brought in as indentured labourers. Some of them became quite well-to-do, owning houses along Argyll Road and driving about in horse-drawn carts. Inevitably, too, the mercantile class scented a good thing and moved in to get their share. Notable were the high caste Nattukkottai Chettiars (mostly from Madras, their name means people with palatial houses in the countryside) whose traditional occupation was money-lending. Before long, they were also providing ready cash to Europeans, Malays and Chinese.

North Indians — that is Punjabis, Gujaratis, Sindhis Bengalis and Bhaiyas from Uttar Pradesh — came a little later though mainly for the same reasons as their brothers from the south. Locals believe that the first Punjabis were brought as policemen by Captain Speedy in 1870. They were among the best Sepoys in the Anglo-Indian army, and remained the most trusted non-commissioned officers even during the Second World War. So there was no question that the British should need a few of them in Penang. Indeed, there were three companies of Sepoys on *HMS Crown* when it sailed to Penang from Calcutta.

As a matter of fact, the first Bengalis in Penang were prisoners and exiles — the remnants of the Punjab army captured when Britain annexed the region after the second Punjab War of 1848. Many of these old soldiers were high-caste officers. The most famous, Maharaj Singh, died in Singapore. His right-hand man, Kharak Singh, was transferred to Penang the following year. Indeed, the last known Bengali prisoner died at the old prison near Sepoy Lines Road. He was believed to have been over a hundred years old, and one night a fierce tropical storm blew over a huge old angsana tree that he'd help to plant when he arrived as a young man. Solemnly regarding the drifts of golden yellow flowers, he told the Malay States Guides who were looking after him, that it was a sign his end was near. He died the next day.

Nevertheless, sufficient numbers of free Punjabis came to Penang of their own accord that by 1803, the Muslim Parthans had their own Bengali Mosque at Leith Street. The non-Muslim Sikhs were granted the honour of having their own *gurdwara* (temple) within Fort Cornwallis itself. Other northern Indians prayed at the Sri Kunj Bihari Temple at Penang Road.

South Indians already had their own places of worship, thanks in part to their spirited womenfolk and Sir George Leith's generosity. In 1801, the Lieutenant-Governor of Penang granted Betty Lingam Chetty a piece of land along the present Queen Street, on which she promptly built the Sri Maha Mariamman temple, though it was only consecrated much later. The next year, the indefatigable Ranee Dhobi (the same laundry queen who sold land to Phillips for his mansion) got an equally impressive piece of real estate at York Close. She must have been as untiring as her name implied since she was wealthy enough to create a trust for the temple known as Ranee Dhobi's Koil before her death. Her shrine existed until 1872 — the Sri Ramar Temple stands in its place now. The Chettiars did not begin constructing their own Arulmigu Thandayuthapani Temple at Waterfall Road until 1854, because they wanted to buy the land for their quarters, the *chettinar*, first.

Most Indian labourers preferred to go home after their contracts expired; their savings amounted to large sums when converted to Indian *rupees*. One group that elected to stay on in Penang was the Telugus. And they had a good reason for that. The men did not come alone — they'd brought their wives and children and preferred to move on to other plantations when their contracts ended.

Another group of Indian migrants, the Malayalees, was largely Muslim. Many intermarried with the Malays and assimilated into the local community successfully. Of those others who chose to stay on, the Malabari workers became famous for their skill and daring. They pioneered some of the most difficult and dangerous techniques in construction and production. After Penang ceased to be a penal colony in 1860, they easily found employment with local Chinese and Indian contractors as well as the Public Works Department and the City Council. A good number went on to become successful contractors themselves. Penang's early tram services, the Funicular Hill Railway, the Sri Mariamman Temple at Air Itam and the Methodist Church were constructed largely by Malabari workers.

By the end of the 19th century, Indian merchants controlled the trade in onions, betel nuts, rice, spices and textiles. Yet it is the efforts and sacrifices of the illiterate newcomers that have made the Indian story in Penang a tale of success. Hole-in-the-wall stallholders, street-side vendors, peddlers, hawkers, bakers, let alone manual labourers, nearly all invested their precious savings in their children's education. Curiously, the first Indian language classes (in Tamil) were not started by the Indians themselves but by the English — at the Penang Free School way back in 1816.

Although the first Tamil school was only opened in 1908 at Nibong Tebal, the *Thangai Nesan* (a Tamil magazine) went into publication as early as 1876. The following year *Sathiya Vedha Sarithira Saaram (The Essence of the Bible)* was published by Palavendhiram Rayappan in Penang. A significant amount of poetry was produced — the list of Penang-based writers and poets is long and comprehensive. In fact, the Penang Tamil Writers Association (formerly the North Malaya Tamil Writers' Association) remains the only such language and community-based literary organization on the isle and there is still no equivalent body for the other races to date, though they have their own reporters and journalists' associations.

It should, therefore, come as no surprise that the Indian community on the island boasts many prominent professionals in its ranks — doctors, surgeons and lawyers, especially. The first Indian

Chamber of Commerce was formed in the 1924; by 1951 Indian investment in Malaya was estimated at around $666 million (three-quarters of which came from the Chettiars). Many of its records were lost during the War, but upon resumption of activities in 1946, a lot of its members went into the entrepôt trade. The Penang Chamber acquired its own premises in 1963, after playing a major role in the formation of the Associated Indian Chambers of Commerce of Malaysia in 1950.

One unexpected consequence of all this economic progress, however, is the vanishing of many time-honoured (if somewhat less cushy) trades. Most of the early businesses that were responsible for moving spices, textiles and other Indian goods across the world no longer exist. The one thing that neither time nor progress has been able to eradicate, however, is the Indians' contribution to the culinary culture of Penang. Over the centuries, Malays, Eurasians and Chinese have developed a fondness for rich, spicy Indian fare and incorporated elements of it into their own cuisines.

The best-loved form of Indian food probably began with a few hawkers patiently trudging from villages to far flung plantations with two baskets of food on a stick slung across each of their shoulders. Hungry planters were probably the first customers for the delicious combination of white rice and rich, fragrant curries which the hawkers had carried for miles, but it didn't take long before the other races wanted a taste of it, too.

Today, the patient old *nasi kandar* man who happily opened up his steaming baskets right in front of your doorstep, has given way to the ubiquitous and fashionable *nasi kandar* restaurant where you have to queue up just to get a plate, but the name (literally rice carried on a yoke) honours his humble memory.

Penang's Serani: The Eurasians

Mr. de Mello, a Eurasian interpreter, was standing beside the Hon. Edward Monkton when he talked terms with the Sultan of Kedah, and Eurasians were there when Light raised the British flag in Penang on 11 August 1786. Moreover it was Francis Xavier Augustin, a Eurasian, who had to climb the pole to dislodge the flag — which had become stuck, with enemy warplanes buzzing in overhead — at the onset of the Japanese invasion of 1941, for the 'E' Eurasian Company men were the only volunteers available when the order came for the Union Jack to be lowered. And, of course, the Eurasians were there when the British returned and yet again, when the Malaysian flag replaced the British standard for the first time ever. Their story, however, began much, much earlier — even before the term Eurasian was coined in 1844.

Originally, Eurasian referred specifically to the child of a white father and an Indian mother. It was meant to differentiate between them and the white British colonialists who had served (some for generations) in India, and who all this time had been lumped together as Anglo-Indians.

Today, however, Eurasian simply means any Asian with one white parent, though it also refers to the peoples of those nations between the two continents. But whereas the mixed Indians shunned it, Penang's Eurasians, who are mainly of Portuguese and Dutch descent and therefore of a much more historic heritage, were happy to embrace the term when it was first applied to them during the 1920s. The Malays and Chinese have always called them Serani — the colloquial form of *nasrani* which meant Christian because they were mostly Roman Catholics, and their story in Penang is closely intertwined with the history of the Church on the island.

When the Portuguese began their voyages of discovery, they were content to accept the children of their intrepid adventurers as citizens. After all, these were the offspring of lusty seafarers, and their small nation needed many strong men if they were to achieve their triple aims of gaining Glory, bringing back Gold and spreading the Gospel — the infamous 3 G's of Portuguese foreign policy.

When Portugal conquered and ruled parts of the Malayan archipelago between 1511 to 1641, they first used the term Luso-Malays (*Luso* from Lusitanian) to refer to their children, though Malacca Portuguese came into general use after that. And these Serani were the founding members and first parishioners when the Portuguese Jesuit Mission led by St. Francis Xavier set up the Catholic Church in Malaya.

Naturally, the coming of the Protestant Dutch was bad news for them. Those who could afford it, fled to the neighbouring Malay states, Sumatra, Macassar, Goa and other Jesuit centres like Phuket, then called Junk Ceylon (a typically European mispronunciation of its Malay name, *Ujong Salang*). Those Catholic Serani who were too poor stayed back and weathered the 154-year storm as best they could — they had to do it all over again, when the Dutch came back between 1814 and 1824. The Eurasians had to conduct their masses secretly in the jungle, yet managed to convert so many of their persecutors through marriage that today, a quarter of the Eurasians in Malaya have Dutch names. They are still predominantly Catholic, however, and have even preserved their sixteenth-century Portuguese customs and language as *lingua de christao* (pronounced christang). But it was those who went to Phuket who were to play a part in the Penang adventure.

These and their Thai-Portuguese counterparts were already well-established when Light came on the scene. They managed the Portuguese factory for trade in elephants and tin, of which there were large deposits. At that period, Kedah claimed possession of Phuket, so Light's de facto wife, Martina Rozells has also been called a Portuguese of Siam and it is quite likely that she had relatives there, though she and her father were residing at the Sultan's court at the time she set out on her mission to seduce the English skipper. Certainly, when the Siamese reasserted their control over the island and massacred the Christians there in 1778, the Thai-Portuguese made the long overland trek to Kedah where Sultan Abdullah most graciously gave them a large house to serve as a church in 1782. There, services were conducted by two French priests, Fathers Coudé and Garnault, in Portuguese and Thai on alternate Sundays.

In the frantic escape to Penang, a number of Thai and former Malacca-Portuguese accompanied the clerics on board Light's ships. As Light needed able, educated men to help in the administration of Penang, they formed the nucleus of his fledgling government. He gave them the piece of land bounded today by Pitt Street, Bishop Street, China Street and Church Street. The remaining Serani were brought over on *Speedwell* on 15 August, the Feast of the Assumption. When Father Garnault built his humble house of worship at Church Street, it followed that he should commemorate the occasion by naming it after that blessed day. Built on a mangrove swamp, constructed of native timber, roofed with attap leaves and standing on spindly stilts, it certainly needed every blessing.

Father Coudé had been made a Bishop even before he boarded Light's ship and when he died, Father Garnault became Superior of the Catholic Mission in Siam and Bishop of Siam and Queda. Still, the French Catholic Mission could hardly have been pleased that the founding parishioners of its revived Catholic Church in Malaya were mainly Portuguese, a number of whom retained their faith in the teachings of the original Portuguese Mission, under the Archbishop of Goa.

Small groups of these Malayan or Thai-Portuguese had come with the traders who used to stop over at Batu Ferringhi and Pulau Tikus, an islet off the coast at Tanjung Bunga. Their homes lay between the two narrow rivers (now covered) that ran through the area bounded by the present Bagan Jermal and Cantonment roads. But the area was not called a Eurasian village until much later because it already bore a much less flattering name — Pulau Tikus or *Rat Island* — since the sand banks, which included the stretch behind modern-day Gurney Drive, resembled the backs of swimming rats at low tide.

It was here that the French Catholic Mission chose to purchase a piece of land even though the latecomers, who were presumably friendlier to them, set up the original Kampung Serani or Eurasian Village around Muntri Street, Love Lane and Argus Lane in Georgetown. And it was on their newly acquired land that the French re-established the College General after the one in Ayutthia was closed down during the Siamese massacres. Set in a tropical paradise of lush fruit and brilliantly blossoming *angsana* trees, the College's new building was meant to train priests for Asian churches. But it looked so dauntingly austere that the fun-loving Portuguese descendants kept their distance, and stayed well outside the two fences which bordered the paths to the seaside.

Their numbers received a boost, however, when the Siamese began slaughtering Catholics again. The remnants of the Phuket community fled the island in 1811. Their parish priest, Father John Pasqual, led them to Pulau Tikus where he had many friends and relatives. His first church there was a small tent with the dead buried all around it —the present Kelawei Road Catholic Cemetery. Eventually, his better-off parishioners gave up their lands around College Lane and Leandros Lane so that he could build the first Church of the Immaculate Conception.

This same group, and their poorer fellow refugees eventually formed the nucleus of the second Kampung Serani at Pulau Tikus, where Father Pasqual built two schools — the Noah's Ark (demolished in 1994) for boys and Pulau Tikus Convent Primary School, which still stands. Sadly, just after conducting his last burial service in 1823, Father John left Penang forever. Exhausted by the constant friction with the French missionaries just across the road from his own church, the old priest returned to Siam where under the kindly King Rama II, Christian missionaries were no longer in danger of their lives.

By then, the Penang Eurasians were in much demand as administrators. They were the most proficient in English, which had replaced Portuguese, Siamese and the local languages as the medium of instruction. Bishop Boucho, parish priest of Father Garnault's old Assumption Church, had opened St. Francis Xavier's Free School (at Bishop Street) and a small girls' school in 1820. At his request in 1852, the La Salle Brothers of the Christian Schools and the Sisters of the Holy Infant Jesus took charge of them. They took over the Pulau Tikus girls' school as well and 150 years later, expanded its premises so that they could also run a secondary school. They also managed to acquire one of Light's former residences, the Navy House, in 1853 — the Light Street Convent School for girls still stands in its original location, while the Brothers moved to Farquhar Street and renamed their school St. Xavier's Institution.

Arguably, the coming of the LaSalle Brothers was a mixed blessing for Penang's Eurasian community. When they established St. Joseph's Novitiate beside the College General opposite Kampung Serani at Pulau Tikus in 1918 and turned it into a

'Training House for Brothers recruited in our schools all over the Far East' the focus shifted from a Eurasian heritage to a Catholic one. As many of the prominent families were moving into government quarters provided by the British administration, both Eurasian villages went into decline. The Rat Island village shrank to the small area between the Church, Leandros Lane, Burmah Road and Kelawei Road (the Millionaire's Row of its day). The George Town kampong was confined to Argus Lane. Nevertheless, the Eurasian community did well. Many were administrators — Sir Hugh Clifford recorded that without their contributions, the Straits Settlements administration might very well have foundered — or entrepreneurs and professionals. Their womenfolk were the backbone of the earliest nursing services. Joseph C. Pasqual, a tin-mining and agricultural expert who wrote many books, had his own column in *The Sunday Times* until he died in 1937.

It was natural that when the British formed Volunteer Corps in the Settlements before World War I the Eurasians should have their own company, as distinct from the Malay, Indian and Chinese ones. There were Penang Eurasians in the British Army, too. Capt. Michael Foley, B. A., of the 10th battalion, Middlesex Regiment, who was killed in action in the Dardanelles, was a Queen's Scholar and an old boy of St. Xavier's.

But when the Japanese overran the peninsula, the *Seranis*' close associations with the British made them suspect. Spied upon and subjected to severe restrictions, they received the ultimate penalty at the slightest hint of suspicion. Dr. Smith, a president of the Penang Eurasian Association, and all his relatives were beheaded on the word of an anonymous informer. So were his friends. They had to dig a long trench, kneel in a row beside it, and then their heads were chopped off one after another. Those members of the Eurasian 'E Company' who survived were given police duties, at which they continued when the British returned.

In the intervening years, so many of the Serani have moved out of their old enclaves that the George Town village is no longer identifiable as a Eurasian area. Nonetheless, the first Malaysian Eurasian parish priest, Father De Silva, was installed in 1950, the Assumption church was elevated to the status of a Cathedral and, five years after that, a Penang-born Bishop was appointed.

The Catholic Church evicted the last members of Pulau Tikus Kampong Serani, against strong opposition led by Regina Pasqual Sibert and Mary Scully Joseph. Regina was 91 years old and Mary 85 when they led their peaceful demonstration in defence of their Eurasian heritage and the poorest Catholic families (which included Chinese and Indians) that still lived there. When Noah's Ark and the other much-loved buildings were flattened in the name of development in 1994, it must have been scant consolation that the original College General nearby was also reduced to rubble.

The Eurasians have done well in Penang. Their homes may scattered all over the island and their social activities as a community less frequent. But they are still so well-regarded that tickets to the Penang Eurasian Society's annual New Year's Eve ball are eagerly sought-after. No one can deny that the Serani throw the best parties!

ACKNOWLEDGEMENTS

Thirty years of visiting Penang have made this book a labour of love. Apart from the expertise of the late Sjovald Cunyngham-Brown, I have been fortunate enough to benefit from the editorial skills of Professor Geoffrey Blainey A.C., the distinguished Australian historian, let alone some poolside comments from Ann Blainey, prize-winning author of I Am Melba and other biographies. Once again the Malaysian writer, Winston Lim, has been most helpful, and I am grateful to Michael and Ann Todd, old-timers in Penang, for their advice. To these good friends my sincere thanks, along with words of appreciation to Dato' Loh Cheng Yean, my co-author of *Tan Sri Loh Boon Siew The Life and Times of a Fire Dragon*, Datuk Winston Tan, Datuk Syed Mohammad Aidid, Edwin and Susan Yap, Watson Chong, Francis Tan, Derek Tan, Laurence and Evelyn Perera, Weena Chua, Ulrich and Gloria Kunzmann, Dr. Jitendra Tejani, Dr. Ramachandran, Laura Joseph, Sherine Tan, Ishwar (Roger), Devi (Dolly) and Premila (Pamela) Budhrani, Sargunathan, as well as the staff of the Casuarina Hotel during the 1980s and from 1990 onwards, the management and staff of the Bayview Beach Resort, for their notable acts of kindness.

SELECT BIBLIOGRAPHY

Raffles of Singapore. Emily Hahn. Aldor. London 1948

Malaysia's First British Pioneer — The Life of Francis Light. Harold P. Clodd. Luzac & Company. 1948

The Golden Chersonese. Isabella L. Bird. Murray. London 1883.

Report from Malaya. Vernon Bartlett. Verschoyle. London 1954.

An Anecdotal History of Old Times in Singapore (1819-1867). C. B. Buckley. Fraser and Neave. Singapore 1902

A History of Malaya. Sir R. O. Winstedt. Malayan Branch, Royal Asiatic Society. Singapore 1935

The Jungle Is Neutral. F. Spencer Chapman. Chatto and Windus. London 1949

Nineteenth Century Malaya. C. D. Cowan. Oxford University Press. London 1961

Malaya. J. M. Gullick. Benn. London 1964

The Story of Malaysia. Harry Miller. Faber. London 1965

Raffles : The Story of Singapore. Raymond Flower. Marshall Cavendish 2007

The Chinese in Penang: A Pictorial History. Tan Kim Hong. *Areca Books, October 2007*

The Gujaratis In The Pearl Of The Orient. Rev. Sumana Siri. Gujarati Sewa Samaj. Penang

The Catholic Church in Malaya. Felix George Lee. Eastern Universities Press Ltd. 1963

A Trip Through Siam. *J. C. Pasqual*. *Penang Gazette Press*. *1900*

Historical Personalities of Penang. Penang State Government. 1986

My *People*, My *Country*. Bernard Sta Maria. The Malacca Portuguese Development Centre, 1982

REFERENCES

Memoir of the Life and Public Services of Sir Thomas Stamford Raffles. Sophia Raffles. James Duncan. London 1835

The Penang Story (a colloquium jointly organised by the Penang Heritage Trust and Star Publications (M) Bhd and sponsored by The Japan Foundation, ABN-AMRO Bank and the State Government in support of Penang's nomination to the World Heritage List together with Malacca). References from papers presented by Datuk Dr. Nazir Ariff, Prof. Dr. Mohd. Razha Rashid, Prof. Ghulam-Sarwar Yousof, director of the Asian Centre of Penang, Prof. Dr. Suresh Narayanan, Professor Dr. Wazir Jahan Karim, Dr. Satish Shukla, Yusuf Azmi Merican, Abdur-Razzaq Lubis, Mohd. Bahroodin Ahmad, Jessica Binwani, S. Seeni Naina Mohamed Hanapi Dollah P. Rajavelan, Taizoon Tyedkhan, K. Thiruvarasu, S. P. Annamalai, Rajinder Singh

The Indonesians in Penang. Paper presented to the Perhimpunan Pelajar Indonesia Kawasan Utara Malaysia, Universiti Sains Malaysia by Abdur-Razzaq Lubis. 2000

Sejarah Johor. Haji Buyong Adil. Dewan Bahasa dan Pustaka

Kurikulum Bersepadu Sekolah Menengah Sejarah Tingkatan 2. Zainal Abidin bin Abdul Wahid, Khoo Kay Kim, Muhd. Yusuf bin Ibrahim, D. S. Ranjit Singh. Dewan Bahasa dan Pustaka. 1994

Chinese Southern Diaspora Studies, Volume 1, 2007. Wong Yeetuan

Indians In Malaya : Some Aspects of the Immigration And Settlement (1786-1957). Kernial Singh Sandhu. Cambridge University Press. London.

Annual Reports of The Malaysian Indian Chamber of Commerce & Industry, Penang from 1948-2000

A Brief History of Indian Business & The Indian Chamber in Penang. Taizoon H. Tyebkhan

Bygone Eurasia. J. F. Augustin. Rajiv Printers, K. L.. (undated)

Portuguese-Eurasian Communities in Southeast Asia. Ronald Daus. Institute of Southeast Asian Studies — Free University of Berlin. 1989

Pulo Ticus 1810-1994, Mission Accomplished. A. E. Sibert. Unpublished manuscripts

Souvenir of the Golden Jubilee of Bro. James, Christian Brothers' Schools 1887-1937 Publication. 1982

The Eurasian Review (July 1934 and March 1937). The Eurasian Associations.

Solid Foundation by Loh Foon Yong in the *Lifestyle* section, *The Star*, 25 March 2009

Encyclopediædia Britanica. 1911 Edition.

www.nationmaster.com/encyclopedia/History-of-modern-Penang

http://magazine.virtualmalaysia.com

http://www.sabrizain.org/malaya

Penang Tourism Action Council,
56th Floor, KOMTAR, 1000 Penang, West Malaysia
Email: *enquiry@tourismpenang.gov.my*

ABOUT THE AUTHOR

When Raymond Flower first visited Penang in 1978, he was so captivated by its unique cultural mix that he has returned regularly every winter and worked on many of is widely-acclaimed books at Batu Ferringhi. These range from historical surveys of Egypt, Italy and Switzerland, Britain—including an official history of Lloyd's of London, as well as the Royal Automobile Club's *Centenary of Motoring*—to various books about Southeast Asia, notably *Raffles: The Story of Singapore* (Marshall Cavendish Editions) and a biography of Loh Boon Siew (written in collaboration with Dato Loh and Winston Lim).

A graduate of Madgalen College, Oxford and an underwriting member of Lloyd's, racing driver. car constructor, international tennis player and Tuscan wine producer, his eventful career is described in *Playback*, which deals with writing an autobiography (SNP Press 2003), not to mention Winston Lim's light-hearted *Car, Castello and Quill* (SNP Press 2007).